Nancy Lindop's Genealogies
Volume 3

Baker, Furnival, Jones
and Shuker

By
Nancy and Geoffrey Lindop

First published 2015

Published by:
Mercianotes
Wigton
CA7 5AQ
United Kingdom

© 2015 Mercianotes

ISBN: 978-1507595527

The Baker Family Tree

The geneaology of a family living in north Shropshire and south Cheshire

By Nancy and Geoffrey Lindop

MERCIANOTES, WIGTON UK

Aaron

76B01   **Aaron Baker**
Baptised 28 December 1766 at Wybunbury
Son of William (72M01) Baker

Alfred

86B01   **Alfred Baker**
Grandson of John (81M01) and Sarah Baker
Son of Jesse (83B01) and Ellen Baker
Born 8 July 1862

Alice

68M01 **Alice** or **Ann Baker** (details on register obscure)
Wife of John (68M01) Baker
  ♂ Thomas (details on register obscure)
Baptised 27 October 1702 at Mucklestone and born in Woore.

70D01   **Alice Baker** of Woore
Buried 7 July 1773 at Mucklestone.

70M02   **Alice Baker**
Second Wife of John (70M01) Baker

  ♂ James (72B01) Baptised 4 July 1725 at Mucklestone and born in Woore.

  ♀ Alice (72B01) Baptised 10 January 1726 at Mucklestone and born in Woore.

  ♀ Ann (72B01) Baptised 13 April 1727 at Mucklestone and born in Woore.

  ♂ John (73B01) Baptised 11 September 1730 at Mucklestone and born in Woore.

72B01   **Alice Baker**
Daughter of John (70M01) and Alice Baker.
Born in Woore 1726.
Baptised 10 January 1726 at Mucklestone.

79B01   **Alice Baker** of Nantwich
Daughter of William Baker (75M01)
Baptised 20 May 1792 in Nantwich.

Ann

72B01   **Ann Baker**
Daughter of John (70M01) and Alice Baker
Born in Woore 1727
Baptised 13 April 1727 at Mucklestone

75B01   **Ann Baker** of Nantwich
Daughter of Peter Baker (72M01)
Baptised 16 February 1752 in Nantwich

81B01   **Ann Baker**
Baptised 22 July 1810 at Wybunbury
Daughter of Thomas Baker (78M01) and Catherine ('Kitty')

81B02   **Ann Baker**
Baptised 5 March 1815 at Wybunbury
Daughter of James Baker (79M01)

84B01   **Ann Baker**
Daughter of William (80B03) and Mary
Born 1847.
1851: living in Checkley

85B01   **Ann Baker**
Great-Grandparents: John Baker (77M01) and Ellen Edwards
Grandparents: John Baker (79B01) and Martha
Parents: Mark Baker (82B01) and Mary Lewis
Born: 1857
Baptised: 12 December 1857 at Maer
Married: John Leighton on 10 May 1880
They had 11 Children

Catherine

75B01   **Catherine Baker** of Nantwich
Daughter of Henry (73M01) Baker
Baptised 25 October 1758 in Wybunbury

75B02   **Catherine Baker** of Nantwich
Daughter of Peter Baker (72M01)
Baptised 16 December 1753 in Nantwich
She must have died an infant because another Catherine (76B01) was born nine years later.

76B01   **Catherine Baker** of Nantwich
Daughter of Peter Baker (72M01)
Baptised 13 January 1762 in Nantwich

Charity

75B01 **Charity Baker**
Daughter of William (72M01) Baker
Baptised 4 March 1754 at Wybunbury

Charles

87M01 **Charles William Baker**
married Alice
♂ Charles Reginald (89B01)

89B01 **Charles Reginald Baker**
Son of Charles William (87M01)
and Alice
Born 1 August 1890

Eli

83B01 **Eli Baker**
Parents: William Baker (80B03)
and Mary Dunn
Baptised: 22 October 1837 at Wybunbury
1851: A farm servant living in Checkley

Elizabeth

62B01 **Elizabeth Baker** of Nantwich
Daughter of William Baker (59M01)
Baptised 11 November 1621 in Nant-
wich.

70M01 **Elizabeth Baker**
First Wife of John (70M01) Baker
Buried: 24 December 1723 at Muckle-
stone.

70M02 **Elizabeth Baker**
Wife of John (77M05) Baker

♂ Peter (77B01) Baptised 12 July 1772
at Mucklestone and born in Woore

♂ John (71D02) Buried 1 July 1781 at
Mucklestone

73B01 **Elizabeth Baker** of Acton
Daughter of Jonas (71M01) and Mary
Baptised 19 September 1731

77B01 **Elizabeth Baker** of Nantwich
Daughter of William Baker (75M01)
Baptised 2 March 1777 in Nantwich.

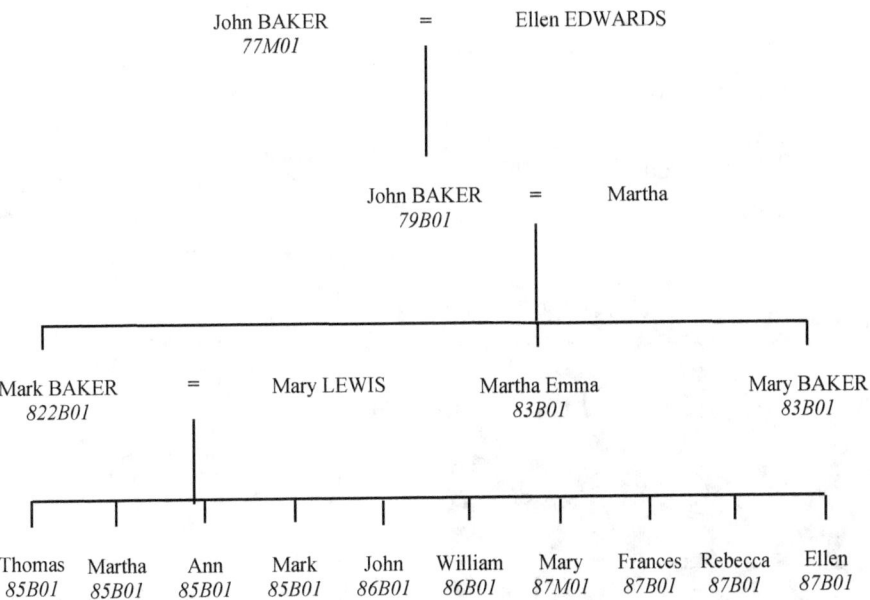

1

78B01 Elizabeth Baker
Baptised 26 November 1780 at Wybunbury
Daughter of Thomas Baker (78M01) and Catherine ('Kitty')

81B01 Elizabeth Baker
Baptised 3 February 1814 at Wybunbury
Daughter of Thomas Baker (78M01) and Catherine ('Kitty')
Sarah's twin sister.

81M02 Elizabeth Baker
Wife of John (81M03) Baker
♂ Thomas (83B01) born and buried 1830

84B01 Elizabeth Baker
Parents: William Baker (80B03) and Mary Dunn
Baptised: 4 May 1845 at Wybunbury

84B02 Elizabeth Baker
Wife of James Baker (84B01)
Maiden Name: Shuker
Born: 11 August 1849 in Bridgemere
Grandaughter of John Shuker
Daughter of John Shuker and Mary Cadman

She married James at the age of 24 in the parish of Haslington by licence. The witnesses were Ebenezer Shuker and Jane Green.

Buried at Wybunbury, 19 February 1928

85B01 Elizabeth Baker
Daughter of John (82B03) and Betsey Baker
Born 11 March 1859 at Wybunbury

Ellen

84M01 Ellen Baker
Wife of Jesse Baker (84M01)
♂ Alfred (86B01) born 8 July 1862

Ellen Baker 87B01

87B01 Ellen Baker
Great-Grandparents: John Baker (77M01) and Ellen Edwards
Grandparents: John Baker (79B01) and Martha
Parents: Mark Baker (82B01) and Mary Lewis
Born: 23 April 1877
Died: 8 June 1964
Married: George Edwin Lindop
Buried: Mucklestone

♂ ♀ Children born after 1900
The picture on the previous page shows white-haired Ellen Lindop (as she then was) standing with her elder son, and his motorbike. Seated is her younger daughter and two of her grandsons. Photo taken at Mount Pleasant, Woore, where she lived in the latter part of her life.

Emily

85B01 Emily Baker
Daughter of John (83M02)and Mary Baker
Born 10 August 1851 at Wybunbury

85B02 Emily Baker
Daughter of William (80B03) and Mary
Born 1852.
1861 living in Checkley (1861 Census)

Enoch

84B01 Enoch Baker
Son of John (81M01) and Sarah Baker
Born 1845

Frances

60B01 Frances Baker of Nantwich
Daughter of John Baker (58M01).
Born in Nantwich 12 March 1605

87B01 Frances Baker
Great-Grandparents: John Baker (77M01) and Ellen Edwards
Grandparents: John Baker (79B01) and Martha
Parents: Mark Baker (82B01) and Mary Lewis
Born: 14 February 1870
Married: 25 January 1897 James Ashcroft Lewis

Francis Baker

87B01

George

74B01 **George Baker** of Nantwich
Son of Peter Baker (72M01)
Baptised 13 September 1749 in Nantwich

77B01 **George Baker** of Nantwich
Son of William Baker (75M01)
Baptised 13 February 1776 in Nantwich

79B01 **George Baker**
Son of John Baker (75M01)
Baptised 5 January 1794 at Wybunbury

83B01 **George Baker**
Parents: William Baker (80B03)
and Mary Dunn
Baptised: 6 March 1836 at Wybunbury
Buried: 14 March 1836

Hannah

74B01 **Hannah Baker**
Daughter of William (72M01) Baker
Baptised 3 May 1744 at Wybunbury

78B01 **Hannah Baker**
Daughter of Thomas Baker (78M01)
and Catherine ('Kitty')
Baptised 22 December 1782 at Wybunbury

78B02 **Hannah Baker** of Nantwich
Daughter of William Baker (75M01)
Baptised 11 September 1785 in Nantwich.

Harriett

84B01 **Harriett Baker**
Daughter of John (81M01) and Sarah Baker
Born 1846 at Wybunbury

Henry

73M01 **Henry Baker** of Nantwich
♀ Catherine (75B01) born 1758
♀ Mary (76B01) born 1769

76M01 **Henry Baker** of Wybunbury
♀ Sarah (78B01) born 1780

James

72B01 **James Baker**
Son of John (70M01) and Alice Baker
Born in Woore 1725
Baptised 4 July 1725 at Mucklestone

78B01 **James Baker**
Son of Thomas Baker (78M01)
and Catherine ('Kitty')
Baptised 16 September 1787 at Wybunbury

78B02 **James Baker**
Son of John Baker (71M01)
Baptised 11 May 1788 at Wybunbury

78B03 **James Baker** of Nantwich
Son of William Baker (75M01)
Baptised 14 April 1782 in Nantwich.

79M01 **James Baker**
A joiner from Walgerton. He married Ann.
♀ Ann (81B02) born 1815 Walgerton
♂ John (81B02) born 1816 Walgerton
♀ Sarah (81B02) born 1819 Walgerton
♀ Martha (81B02) born 1821 Walgerton

80B01 **James Baker**
Son of Thomas Baker (78M01)
and Catherine ('Kitty')
Baptised 23 June 1805 at Wybunbury

84B01 **James Baker**
Parents: William Baker (80B03) and Mary
Dunn
Baptised: 3 September 1844 at Wybunbury
1851 living in Checkley
1861 living in Checkley
1871 living in Checkley and working as a
wheelwright
Married Elizabeth Shuker 12 August 1873 in
the Parish of Haslington. He was a
wheelwright at Doddington at that
time.

He lived at Cherry Tree Farm.
1892: A Carpenter at Checkley
Buried Wybunbury 29 June 1924

88B01 **James Newton Baker**
Baptised 17 February 1886 at Wybunbury

Jane

78B01 **Jane Baker**
Daughter of John Baker (75M01)
Baptised 9 January 1782 at Wybunbury

Jesse

83B01   **Jesse Baker**
Son of John (81M01) and Sarah Baker
Born 1839 at Wybunbury
Married Ellen
♂ Alfred (86B01) born 8 July 1862

John

58M01   **John Baker** of Nantwich
♀ Frances (60B01), was born 12 March 1605/6

63D01   **John Baker** of Woore
Buried September 1704 at Mucklestone

65M01   **John Baker** of Acton
♂ John (67B01) baptised 1 September 1673
♂ Thomas (67B01) baptised 7 February 1675/6

67B01   **John Baker** of Acton
Son of John Baker (65M01)
Baptised 1 September 1673 in Acton

68M01   **John Baker**
Married Ann or Alice (details on register obscure)
♂ Thomas Baptised 27 October 1702 at Mucklestone and born in Woore

70M01   **John Baker** of Woore
Husbandman
Married (1) Elizabeth (70M01)
    No children
Married (2) Alice (70M02)

♂ James (72B01) Baptised 4 July 1725 at Mucklestone and born in Woore

♀ Alice (72B01) Baptised 10 January 1726/7 at Mucklestone and born in Woore

♀ Ann (72B01) Baptised 13 April 1727 at Mucklestone and born in Woore

♂ John (73B01) Baptised 11 September 1730 at Mucklestone and born in Woore

Buried 23 April 1743 at Mucklestone.

71D02   **John Baker**
Son of John and Elizabeth Baker. He could be the son of John (77M05) and Elizabeth.

Buried 1 July 1781 at Mucklestone

73B01   **John Baker**
Son of John (70M01) and Alice Baker
Born in Woore 1730
Baptised 11 September 1730 at Mucklestone

75M01   **John Baker** of Wybunbury
♂ John (77B03) Baptised 31 October 1773
♂ John (77B04) Baptised 3 September 1776
♂ Thomas (77B01) Baptised 24 May 1779
♀ Jane (78B01) Baptised 9 January 1782
♂ James (78B02) Baptised 5 November 1788
♂ George (79B01) Baptised 5 January 1794
♂ John (79B02) Baptised 30 March 1796

77M01   **John Baker** of Stoke on Trent
Married: Ellen Edwards 25 April 1791 at Stoke on Trent. The marriage was witnessed by Samuel Poulson and Samuel Johnson

♂ John (79B01) born 1792

77B02   **John Baker**
Son of Thomas Baker (78M01)
    and Catherine ('Kitty')
Baptised 10 August 1777 at Wybunbury

77B03   **John Baker**
Son of John Baker (71M01)
Baptised 31 October 1773 at Wybunbury
It is assumed that John died an infant, since another John was born three years later (see 77B04 below).

77B04   **John Baker**
Son of John Baker (71M01)
Baptised 3 September 1776 at Wybunbury
It is assumed that John died an infant, since another John was born twenty years later (see 79B02 below).

77M05 John Baker of Woore
Married Elizabeth (70M02)

  ♂ Peter (77B01) Baptised 12 July 1772 at Mucklestone and born in Woore

  ♂ John (71D02) Buried 1 July 1781 at Mucklestone

78B01 John Baker of Nantwich
Son of William Baker (75M01)
Baptised 8 June 1778 in Nantwich.

79B01 John Baker
Parents: John Baker (77M01) & Ellen Edwards
Born in Stoke on Trent
Baptised: 13 May 1792
Married: Martha

  ♂ Mark (82B01)
  ♀ Martha Emma (83B01)
  ♀ Mary (83B01)

  1851: John was a widower at the age of 58 when he lived with his son Mark at Maer.

79B02 John Baker
Son of John Baker (71M01)
Baptised 20 March 1796 at Wybunbury

79M03 John Baker of Nantwich
Married Mary

  ♀ Mary Astles (81B01), was born 10 September 1812

80M01 John Baker
married Hannah
John was a carpenter in Bridgemere.
  ♂ John (82B01) baptised on 30 May 1824.

80B02 John Baker
Son of Thomas Baker (78M01) and Catherine ('Kitty')
Baptised 7 February 1802 at Wybunbury

80M03 John Baker
Married Margaret
John was a joiner in Hatherton.
  ♂ Robert was baptised on 29 January 1820.

81M01 John Baker
Married Sarah at Wybunbury

81B02 John Baker
Son of James Baker (79M01)
Baptised 25 October 1816 at Wybunbury

81M03 John Baker
Married Elizabeth (81M02)
John was a carpenter in Woore.
  ♂ Thomas (83B01) born and buried 1830

82B01 John Baker
son of John (80M01) and Hannah
Born in Bridgemere
Baptised 30 May 1824 at Wybunbury

82B03 John Baker
Born Hunsterson, nr Wybunbury 1824
Married Betsey (Elizabeth)
  ♂ John (85B01) Born 1852 in Wybunbury
  ♂ Thomas (85B02) Born 1854 inWybunbury
  ♂ William (85B01) Born 1856 in Wybunbury
  ♀ Elizabeth (85B01) Born 1859 in Wybunbury
  ♂ Richard (86B02) Born 1863 in Wybunbury

  1871 Census describes John as a cartpenter. There is no mention in the 1871 Census of Elizabeth who would be 12-year old, nor of William who would be 15. It is assumed that both died in infancy. The eldest son, John was an apprentice pattern maker in 1871 and had left home by 1881.

  1881 Census describes John as a joiner living at 6, Bridge Street, Wybunbury. His two sons, Thomas and Richard were also joiners/carpenters living and presumably working with their father.

John's wife, Betsey, was born 1829 in Whitchurch, Shropshire. The 1871 and 1881 Census returns for her sons John and Thomas prove that her real name was Elizabeth.

83M02 John Baker of Wybunbury
Married Mary

85B01 John Baker
Son of John (83M01) and Elizabeth ("Betsey")
Born 1851 in Wybunbury

  1871 Census describes John as unmarried and an apprentice pattern maker. He had left home by the 1881 Census.

86B01 John Baker
Great-Grandparents: John Baker (77M01)
and Ellen Edwards
Grandparents: John Baker (79B01) &
Martha
Parents: Mark Baker (82B01) and Mary
Lewis
Baptised: 13 April 1862 at Maer

Married (1): <small>wife's name not known</small>
♀ Mabel (89B01) born 1891
♂ Mark (89B01) born 1895

He was a farmer at the Greaves, near
Woore

Married (2): Sarah Ann Boote of Malpas
♂ ♀ Children born after 1900

89M01 John Baker
Great-Great-Grandparents: John Baker
(77M01) and
Ellen Edwards
Great-Grandparents: John Baker (79B01)
and Martha
Grandparents: Mark Baker (82B01)
and Mary Lewis
Father: Mark Baker (85B01)
Born: 1870-1894 possibly 1890
Married: Frances Mitchell on 2 June 1912
They had no children.

Jonas

71M01 Jonas Baker of Acton
Married Mary
♀ Elizabeth (73B01) baptised 19 Sept.
1731

Joseph

79B01 Joseph Baker
Son of Thomas Baker (78M01)
and Catherine ('Kitty')
Baptised 17 February 1793 at Wybunbury

82B01 Joseph Baker
Born 1827 in Minshall Vernon
1851 an agricultural labourer living in
Mosside

Married Martha who was born in 1828.

They could be the niece and nephew of
James and Mary Leigh.

Levi

85B01 Levi Baker
Baptised 10 August 1851 in Wybunbury

Mabel

89B01 Mabel Baker
Great-Great-Grandparents: John Baker
(77M01)
and Ellen Edwards
Great-Grandparents: John Baker (79B01)
and Martha
Grandparents: Mark Baker (82B01)
and Mary Lewis
Parents: John Baker (86B01) by his first
wife
Born: 1891

Started Woore School: 1 March 1897
(age 6) Admission number 711
Left school: July 1905 (age 14)

Married into the Hampson family
♂ ♀ Children born after 1900.

Margaret

74B01 Margaret Baker
Daughter of William (72M01) Baker
Baptised 2 February 1749 at Wybunbury

Mark Baker 82B01

Mark

82B01 Mark Baker
Grandparents: John Baker (77M01)
and Ellen Edwards
Parents: John Baker (79B01) and Martha
Baptised: 23 March 1828 at Stoke on
Trent

1851: He was at Maer where his widowed
father lived with him.

Married: Mary Lewis in 1851
♂ Thomas (85B01) born 1851.
♀ Martha (85B01) born 1852 in Maer
♀ Ann (85B01) born 1857 in Maer
♂ Mark (85B01) born 1859 in Maer
♂ John (86B01) born 1862
♂ William (86B01) born 1864 in Maer
♀ Mary (87M01) born in Ashley some-
time between 1864-1870
♀ Frances (87B01) born 1870
♂ William (85B01) Born 1856 in Wybun-
bury
♀ Elizabeth (85B01) Born 1859 in
Wybunbury
♀ Rebecca (87B01) born 1874
♀ Ellen (87B01) born 1877

1871: The census showed that he was
farming at Rose Cottage, Mill Hill,
Ashley at the age of 42 (he was
therefore born in 1829 or early
1828)
1880: Still farming at Ashley
1880 (October): He farmed at Sillenhurst,
Woore

Married: Mary?
Mary was buried 4 October 1897 aged 68
years. She was born in 1829 in Market
Drayton. *She was the wife of Mark Baker,
but not clear if this is the Mark in ques-
tion.*

Mark was buried on 5 January 1898 aged
71.

John Baker
79B01

(Mark's father)

85B01 Mark Baker
Great-Grandparents: John Baker (77M01)
and Ellen Edwards
Grandparents: John Baker (79B01) &
Martha
Parents: Mark Baker (82B01) and Mary
Lewis
Baptised: 13 October 1859 at Maer
Married: details not known

♀ Pattie (89E01)
♂ John (89M01)
♀ Sarah (89M01)

Farmed at Hookgate
Died before 1914

89B01 Mark Baker
Parents: John Baker (86B01) by his first
wife
Born: 8 March 1895
Started Woore Schoool 2 April 1900
Admission number 732
Left School 11 March 1909 (age 14)
Married: Ginnie
♂ ♀ Children born after 1900.

Martha

75B01 Martha Baker
Daughter of William (72M01) Baker
Baptised 1 January 1757 at Wybunbury

77B01 Martha Baker of Nantwich
Daughter of William Baker (75M01)
Baptised 31 October 1779 in Nantwich.

79M01 Martha Baker
Wife of William (79M02) Baker
Maiden Name: Hitchen
Married on 7 May 1816 at Mucklestone.
Witnessed by: Mary Griffiths
and William Hulme

80B01 Martha Baker
Born 26 April 1803 at Checkley (The
year could be 1903)

81B01 Martha Baker
Daughter of James Baker (79M01)
Baptised 24 June 1821 at Wybunbury

83B01 Martha Emma Baker
Grandparents: John Baker (77M01)
and Ellen Edwards
Parents: John Baker (79B01) and Martha
Baptised: 15 March 1838
at St. Paul's. Burslem

7

84B01 Martha Dunn Baker

Parents: William Baker (80B03) and
Mary Dunn
Baptised: 26 September 1841 at
Wybunbury

1851 living in Checkley

Married James Silvester on 8 August
1862 at Wybunbury. Witness: Eli Baker

85B01 Martha Baker

Great-Grandparents: John Baker (77M01)
and Ellen Edwards
Grandparents: John Baker (79B01) &
Martha
Parents: Mark Baker (82B01) and Lydia
Lewis
Born: 1852 at Maer

Married: 22 March 1871 to John Matthews
After she was marrried she moved to
Buerton where John was an agricultural
labourer.

♀ Mary (87E01)
♀ Fanny (87E01)
♂ Samuel (87E01)
♀ Annie (87E01) There is an element of
doubt if Annie was part of this family
♂ Charles (87E01)
♂ Joseph (87E01)
♀ Nellie (87E01)
♀ Kitty (87E01)
♀ Pattie (87E01)
♀ Hannah (87E01)

Mary

76B01 Mary Baker of Nantwich

Daughter of Henry (73M01) Baker
baptised 17 February 1769 in Wybunbury

78B01 Mary Baker of Nantwich

Daughter of William Baker (75M01)
Baptised 27 December 1789 in Nantwich.

81B01 Mary Astles Baker of Nantwich

Daughter of John (79M03) and Mary
Baker
Born 10 September 1812

81B02 Mary Baker

Wife of William Baker (80B03)
Maiden Name: Dunn
Born in 1810
♂ George (83B01) born 1836 baptised at
Wybunbury
♂ Eli (83B01) born 1837 baptised at
Wybunbury
♂ William (83B01) born 1839 baptised
at Wybunbury
♀ Martha Dunn (83B01) born 1841 bap-
tised at Wybunbury
♂ James (83B01) born 1844 baptised at
Wybunbury
♀ Elizabeth (83B01) baptised at Wybun-
bury
♀ Mary E. (84B01) born 1845 baptised
at Wybunbury
♀ Ann (84B01) born 1847 baptised at
Wybunbury
♀ Emily (85B02) Born 1852 at Checkley
baptised at Wybunbury

1851: The following Children are record-
ed in the 1851 Census (ages in 1851):
Eli (13) born 1838
Martha (9) born 1842
James (7) born 1844
Mary E (6) born 1845
Ann (4) born 1847

1861: The 1861 census also records the
family. Martha and Mary are no longer
living at home. James is a wheelwright,
Ann a servant and Emily, a scholar of 9
years of age in 1861 was not born at the
time of the previous census.

1871 census records that Mary Baker was
a widow living in Checkley.

82B01 Mary Baker

Born: 1829
Buried: 4 October 1897 aged 68
She was from Syllenhurst, Woore

83B01 Mary Baker

Grandparents: John Baker (77M01)
and Ellen Edwards
Parents: John Baker (79B01) and Martha
Baptised: 31 March 1839
in St Paul's, Burslem

84B01 Mary E. Baker

Daughter of William (80B03) and Mary
Born 1845.
1851 living in Checkley

87M01 **Mary Baker**
Great-Grandparents: John Baker (77M01) and Ellen Edwards
Grandparents: John Baker (79B01) & Martha
Parents: Mark Baker (82B01) and Lydia Lewis
Born: born in Ashley sometime between 1864-1870
Married: 6 January 1890 to William Stanyer Major (a Pump maker at Woore)

♂ William Mark (89B01)
♀ Francis Mary (90B01)

Moses

76B01 **Moses Baker**
Son of William (72M01) Baker
Baptised 14 July 1760 at Wybunbury

Pattie

89E01 **Pattie Baker**
Great-Great-Grandparents: John Baker (77M01)
and Ellen Edwards
Great-Grandparents: John Baker (79B01) & Martha
Grandparents: Mark Baker (82B01) & Lydia Lewis
Parents: Mark Baker (85B01)

Born: 1870-1894 possibly 1890
Married: Sid Edwards
♂ ♀ Children born after 1900 are not included in this book.

Peter

72M01 **Peter Baker** of Nantwich
♂ George (74B01) baptised 13 Sept. 1749
♀ Ann (75B01) baptised 16 February 1752
♀ Catherine (75B02) baptised 16 Dec. 1753
♂ Peter (74B01) baptised 8 September 1759
♀ Catherine (76B01) baptised 13 Jan. 1762

75B01 **Peter Baker** of Nantwich
Son of Peter Baker (72M01)
Baptised 8 September 1759 in Nantwich

77B01 **Peter Baker**
Son of John (77M05) and Elizabeth Baker
Born in Woore 1772

Rebecca

87B01 **Rebecca Baker**
Great-Grandparents: John Baker (77M01) and Ellen Edwards
Grandparents: John Baker (79B01) & Martha
Parents: Mark Baker (82B01) & Lydia Lewis
Born: 2nd September 1874

Started Woore School 5 December 1881
Admission number 270
Left school for home 11 May 1888

Married: Percy John Edwards on 18 Oct. 1910
After she was married she lived at the Grange, Gravenhunger

Rhoda

85B01 **Rhoda Baker**
Daughter of John (81M01) and Sarah Baker
Born 1857 at Wybunbury

Richard

61B01 **Richard Baker** of Nantwich
Son of William Baker (59M01)
Baptised 17 December 1616 in Nantwich

81B01 **Richard Baker**
Son of Thomas Baker (78M01)
and Catherine ('Kitty')
Baptised 21 July 1816 at Wybunbury

86M01 **Richard Baker** of Wybunbury
Married Sarah

86B02 Richard Baker
  Son of John (83M01)
  and Elizabeth ("Betsey") Baker
  Born 1863 in Wybunbury

  1871 aged 8 in the Wybunbury census
  1881 described as an 18-year old joiner in
    the 1881 Census.

Robert

81B01 Robert Baker
  Son of Thomas Baker (78M01)
  and Catherine ('Kitty')
  Baptised 16 February 1812 at Wybunbury

82B01 Robert Baker
  Son of John and Margaret of Hatherton.
  Baptised on 29 January 1820 at Wybunbury

Rowland

89B01 Rowland James Baker
  Son of James Baker (84B01)
  and Elizabeth Shuker
  Born 13 June 1890
  Started at Woore School: 13 May 1895
  Married Jessie May Lea 22 July 1928
  ♀ Daughter born after 1900

  He was a motor Proprietor

Samuel

80B01 Samuel Baker
  Son of Thomas Baker (78M01)
  and Catherine ('Kitty')
  Baptised 8 November 1807 at Wybunbury

Sarah

78B01 Sarah Baker
  Daughter of Henry (76M01),
  Baptised on 26 March 1780 at Wybunbury.

81B01 Sarah Baker
  Daughter of Thomas Baker (78M01)
  and Catherine ('Kitty')
  Baptised 3 February 1814 at Wybunbury
  Elizabeth's twin sister.

81B02 Sarah Baker
  Daughter of James Baker (79M01)
  Baptised 25 July 1819 at Wybunbury

83B01 Sarah Baker
  Born 1830 in Malpas
  1851: The census records her as an agri-
    cultural labourer living in Mosside

89M01 Sarah Baker
  Parents: Mark Baker (85B01)
  Born: 1870-1896 possibly 1890
  Married: Ben Salt on 23 March 1914
  Lived at Cherry Tree Farm, Ashley
  ♂ ♀ Children born after 1900

Thomas

67B01 Thomas Baker of Acton
  Son of John Baker (65M01)
  Baptised 7 February 1675 in Acton

70B01 Thomas Baker
  Son of John (68M01) and A. Baker
  Born in Woore 1702
  Baptised 27 October 1702 at Mucklestone

75B01 Thomas Baker
  Son of William (72M01) Baker
  Baptised 1 January 1752 at Wybunbury

77B01 Thomas Baker
  Son of John Baker (71M01)
  Baptised 20 March 1796 at Wybunbury

78M01 Thomas Baker of Wybunbury
  Married Catherine ('Kitty')

  There are problems with this pedigree.
  There are an unusually large number of
  children born over a period of 39 years
  and many children's names are duplicat-
  ed. One theory is that Catherine and Kitty are different people. It could also be
  possible that two Thomas Bakers are in-
  volved. All the baptisms took place at
  Wybunbury. The following is an attempt
  to resolve the issue:

Catherine's Children
♂ John (77B02) Baptised 10 August 1777
♀ Elizabeth (78B01) Baptised 26 Nov. 1780
♀ Hannah (78B01) Baptised 22 Dec. 1782
♂ James (78B01) Baptised 16 Sept. 1787
♂ William (78B01) Baptised 16 August 1789
♂ Joseph (79B01) Baptised 17 Feb. 1793

Kitty's Children
♂ Thomas (80B01) Baptised 28 Dec. 1800
♂ John (80B02) Baptised 7 February 1802
♂ William (80B01) Baptised 6 Nov. 1803
♂ James (80B01) Baptised 23 June 1805
♂ Samuel (80B01) Baptised 8 Nov. 1807
♀ Ann (81B01) Baptised 22 July 1810
♂ Robert (81B01) Baptised 16 Feb. 1812
♀ Sarah (81B01) Baptised 3 February 1814
♀ Elizabeth (81B01) Baptised 3 Feb. 1814
♂ Richard (81B01) Baptised 21 July 1816

78M02 **Thomas Baker** of Wybunbury
Married Hannah

80B01 **Thomas Baker**
Son of Thomas Baker (78M01) and Catherine ('Kitty')
Baptised 28 December 1800 at Wybunbury

83B01 **Thomas Baker**
Son of John (81M03) and Elizabeth (81M02)
Baptised 15 August 1830 at Mucklestone
Buried 17 October 1830 at Mucklestone

85B01 **Thomas Baker**
Great-Grandparents: John Baker (77M01) and Ellen Edwards
Grandparents: John Baker (79B01) & Martha
Parents: Mark Baker (82B01) and Fanny
Born: 1851

A bachelor, he lived with the Majors, who were pump makers in Woore

85B02 **Thomas Baker**
Son of John (83M01) and Elizabeth
Born 1853 in Wybunbury

1871: The Census records that he was un-married and worked as a carpenter.

1881: He remained unmarried in 1881 at the age of 27 and still lived at home (6, Bridge Street, Wybunbury).

William

59M01 **William Baker** of Nantwich

♂ Richard (61B01) Baptised 17 December 1616 in Nantwich
♀ Elizabeth (62B01) Baptised 11 November 1621 in Nantwich

72M01 **William Baker** of Wybunbury
♀ Hannah (74B01) born 1744
♂ William (74B01) born 1746
♀ Margaret (74B01) born 1749
♂ Thomas (75B01) born 1751
♀ Charity (75B01) born 1754
♀ Martha (75B01) born 1756
♂ Moses (76B01) born 1760
♂ Aaron (76B01) born 1766

74B01 **William Baker**
Son of William (72M01) Baker
Baptised 30 September 1746 at Wybunbury

75M01 **William Baker** of Nantwich
Married Anna or Hannah
Their children were baptised in Nantwich:
♂ George (77B01) Baptised 13 Feb. 1776
♀ Elizabeth (77B01) Baptised 2 March 1777
♂ John (78B01) Baptised 8 June 1778
♀ Martha (77B01) Baptised 31 October 1779
♂ James (78B03) Baptised 14 April 1782
♀ Mary (78B01) Baptised 27 Dec. 1789
♀ Hannah (78B02) Baptised 11 Sept. 1785
♀ Alice (79B01) Baptised 20 May 1792
♂ William (79B01) Baptised 31 Dec. 1797

78B01 **William Baker**
Son of Thomas Baker (78M01) and Catherine ('Kitty')
Baptised 16 August 1789 at Wybunbury

79B01 William Baker of Nantwich
Son of William Baker (75M01)
Baptised 31 December 1797 in Nantwich.

79M02 William Baker
Married Martha (79M01) Hitchen on 7
May 1816 at Mucklestone. Witnessed
by: Mary Griffiths and William Hulme

80B01 William Baker
Son of Thomas Baker (78M01)
Baptised 6 November 1803 at Wybun-
bury

80B02 William Baker
Grandson of John Baker (71M01)
Son of Jane Baker (78B01)
Baptised 20 March 1796 at Wybunbury

80B03 William Baker
Born 1802 at Hough.
Married: Mary (81B02) Dunn 28 Febru-
ary 1835 at Wybunbury. Mary was born
in 1810. The wedding was witnessed by
Samual Sherwin and Martha Dunn.
All their children were baptised at
Wybunbury
♂ George (83B01) born 1836
♂ Eli (83B01) born 1837
♂ William (83B01) born 1839
♀ Martha Dunn (83B01) born 1841
♂ James (83B01) born 1844
♀ Elizabeth (83B01) born 1845
♀ Mary E. (84B01) born 1845
♀ Ann (84B01) born 1847
♀ Emily (85B02) Born 1852 at Checkley

1851: The census records him as a labour-
er living in Checkley. The following
Children are recorded in the 1851 Cen-
sus (ages in 1851):
Eli (13) born 1838
Martha (9) born 1842
James (7) born 1844
Mary E (6) born 1845
Ann (4) born 1847

1860: William is listed in a directory as
living at Checkley cum Wrinehill.

1861: This census also records the family.
Martha and Mary are no longer living at
home. James is a wheelwright, Ann a
servant and Emily, a scholar of 9 years
of age in 1861 was not born at the time
of the previous census.

William died sometime between 1861-71
as the 1871 census records that Mary
was a widow living in Checkley.

82B01 William Baker
Born 1827 in Leighton
1851: He is an agricultural labourer living in Mosside.

83B01 William Baker
Parents: William Baker (80B03) & Mary
Dunn
Baptised: 27 October 1839 at Wybunbury

1841: Census records William's age as 12
months, but he is not recorded in the
1851 Census.

85B01 William Baker
Son of John (83M01) and Elizabeth ("Be-
tsey")
Born 1856
William is not mentioned in the 1871
Census.

86B01 William Baker
Great-Grandparents: John Baker (77M01)
and Ellen Edwards
Grandparents: John Baker (79B01) &
Martha
Parents: Mark Baker (82B01) & Lydia
Lewis
Baptised: 24 January 1864 at Maer

Willam was the last of the family to be
born at Maer before they moved to Ashley. *His father farmed at Sillenhurst near
Woore; at Flash near Woore; and finally
at College Fields Cottage near Woore.*

Married: Julia

88C01 William Baker
Lived at Harding Street, Crewe in 1881

The Furnival Family Tree

By Nancy and Geoffrey Lindop

Alice

86B01 Alice Martha Furnival
Great-Grandparents: William Furnival
(75B01) and Hannah Barker
Grandparents: Daniel Furnival (79B01)
and Ann Heywood
Parents: Stephen Furnival (82B01) and
Fanny Bourne
born: 1866
Married J E Bourne.

Ann, Anne or Annie

79B01 Ann Furnival of Napley Heath
Born 1799
Buried at Mucklestone 8 December 1846
aged 47 years.

79B02 Ann Furnival
Parents: Thomas Furnival (76B01) and
Mary Cadman
Born: 1795 Baptised: 24 April 1795
(Moreton Say?)
Married John Spragg of Ridgewardine

81B01 Ann Furnival
Parents: William Furnival (78M01) and
Elizabeth
Born: 1818
Baptised 31 May 1818 in Mucklestone.

82B01 Anne Furnival of Dorrington
Born 1824
Buried at Mucklestone 10 May 1846 aged 22

83B01 Ann Marjory Furnival
Grandparents: William Furnival (75B01)
and Hannah Barker
Parents: Daniel Furnival (79B01) and
Ann Heywood
born 1830
Married William Mate of Norton in Hales
13 May 1858.

Anne Furnival see Mary Anne Furnival (84B01)
Ann Furnival see Elizabeth Ann Furnival (85B01)

86B01 Annie Elizabeth Furnival
Great-Grandparents: William Furnival
(75B01) and Hannah Barker
Grandparents: Daniel Furnival (79B01)
and Ann Heywood
Parents: Stephen Furnival (82B01) and
Fanny Bourne
Born: 1861
Married William Rodenhurst

Betsey Furnival

85B01 Betsey Furnival
Great-Grandparents: William Furnival
(75B01) and Hannah Barker
Grandparents: William Furnival (78B03)
and Sarah Tweed
Parents: Daniel Furnival (81B01) and
Sarah Ridgway
Born: 1855
Baptised 23 October 1855 presumably at
Norton-in-Hales

Charles Furnival

68D01 Charles Furwood
Buried at Mucklestone 1 Sept 1757, the
son of John Furwood (66E01) of Knighton.
The origins of the family are lost in the
mists of time. Assuming the surname
was misspelt by the clerk, an obscure
link may be with John Furwood(66E01)
of Knighton, which is close to Napley
Heath. He had a son Charles Furwood
(68D01) who was buried at Mucklestone
1 Sept 1757. Assuming Charles was 70
when he died, and that John was 20
when Charles was born. John would be
born circa 1680. It is just possible that
the Furwoods headed the Furnival family
tree, but not a lot of faith can be placed
on this assumption.

Daniel Furnival

76B01 Daniel Furnival
Grandparents: William Furnival (70M01)
and Cassandra Wright
Parents: John Furnival (73B01) and Mary
Born: 1764
Baptised: 29 May 1764 at Moreton Say

79B01 Daniel Furnival
Parents: William Furnival (75B01) and
Hannah Barker
Born 1792 at Napley Heath. He was bap-
tised at Mucklestone 21 October 1792
Died 1848 at Napley Heath and was bur-
ied at Mucklestone 10 March 1848 aged
56 years.
Married Ann Heywood of Napley Farm
in 1818
The Roy Furnival Archive records that
Daniel married Ann Highfield, daughter
of John and Margery of Knighton.
Some confusion exists as to which mother
had the following children
John (82B01) born: 1820
Stephen (82B01) born: 1822

Daniel (82B01) born: 1824
James (82B01) born: 1826
Edward (82B01) born: 1828
Ann Marjory (83B01) born: 1830
Martha (83B01) born: 1833
William (83B01) born: 1835
Hannah Eliza (83B01) born: 1836
Elizabeth (83B01) born: 1838
Mary (83B01) born: 1839
Edward (84B01) born: 1840
Sarah (84B01) born: 1842
Henry (84B01) born: 1844
John Daniel (84B01) born: 1846

81B01   Daniel Furnival
Grandparents: William Furnival (75B01)
and Hannah Barker
Parents: William Furnival (78B03)
and Sarah Tweed
Born 1817
Baptised at Mucklestone 12 October 1817
He was a labourer.
.He married Sarah Ridgway, daughter of
Joseph Ridgway and had the following
children.
Betsey (85B01) born: 1855
Henry (85B02) born: 1857
Ellen (85B01) born: 1858

82B01   Daniel Furnival
Grandparents: William Furnival (75B01)
and Hannah Barker
Parents: Daniel Furnival (79B01) and
Ann Heywood
Born 1824
Died 1844 of tuberculosis at Napley
Heath aged 19 and was buried at Muck-
lestone on 25 April 1844.

Daniel Furnival see John Daniel Furnival (84B01)

Doris Furnival

88E01   Doris May Furnival
Great-Great-Grandparents: William Furnival (75B01) and Hannah Barker
Great-Grandparents: Daniel Furnival
(79B01) and Ann Heywood
Grandparents: Stephen Furnival (82B01)
and Fanny Bourne
Parents: John Stephen Furnival (85B01)
and May Bourne

Edith Furnival

87B01   Edith Mary Furnival
Great-Grandparents: William Furnival
(75B01) and Hannah Barker
Grandarents: Daniel Furnival (79B01)
and Ann Heywood
Parents: Stephen Furnival (82B01) and
Fanny Bourne
Born: 1871
Married Harry Cook

Edward Furnival

82B01   Edward Furnival
Grandparents: William Furnival (75B01)
and Hannah Barker
Parents: Daniel Furnival (79B01) and
Ann Heywood
Born: 1828
Baptised: 15 June 1828
Died: 1830 (aged 2)
Buried: 7 February 1830

84B01   Edward Furnival
Grandparents: William Furnival (75B01)
and Hannah Barker
Parents: Daniel Furnival (79B01) and
Ann Heywood
Born 8 December 1840
Married Helen Hordley
Little is known of this pedigree. If Ed-
ward married when he was 20, then their
first daughter, Eva, would have been 20
when she married in 1900.
They had the following children:
Eva Mary (86M01)
Margery (86E02)
Hurdley (86E01) = Elsie
Billy (86E04)

88E01   Ted (Edward) Furnival
Great-Grandparents: William Furnival
(75B01) and Hannah Barker
Grandparents: Daniel Furnival (79B01)
and Ann Heywood
Parents: Hurdley (86E01) and Elsie but
no more details available.

Edwin Furnival

85B01   Edwin Henry Furnival
Great-Grandparents: William Furnival (75B01) and Hannah Barker
Grandparents: Daniel Furnival (79B01) and Ann Heywood
Parents: Stephen Furnival (82B01) and Fanny Bourne
Born: 1855 and baptised at Mucklestone 6 January 1855
Married Elizabeth 'Lizzie' Meakin in 1879, daughter of William Meakin (deceased) of Lea Head
Buried 24 September 1913 (or 1918)
Lived at Bellaport Park Farm, then, according to the 1896 edition of Kelly's Directory, 1896 at Tudley Farm.

88E01   Edwin Bourne Furnival
Great-Great-Grandparents: William Furnival (75B01) and Hannah Barker
Great-Grandparents: Daniel Furnival (79B01) and Ann Heywood
Grandparents: Stephen Furnival (82B01) and Fanny Bourne
Parents: John Stephen Furnival (85B01) and May Bourne

Eliza Furnival

78B02   Eliza Ellen Furnival
Parents: William Furnival (75B01) and Hannah Barker
Born 1787 at Napley Heath
'Elin' was baptised on 24 June 1787 at Mucklestone
Married 1809

Eliza Furnival see Hannah Eliza Furnival (83B01)

83B01   Eliza Furnival
Grandparents: Thomas Furnival (76B01) and Mary Cadman
Parents: Thomas Furnival (80B01) and Eliza
Born: 1833

Eliza Furnival see Fanny Eliza Furnival (86B01)

Elizabeth Furnival

78B01   Elizabeth Furnival
Parents: William Furnival (75B01) and Hannah Barker
Born 1785 at Napley Heath in the parish of Mucklestone. She was baptised in the parish church on 3rd July 1785

79B01   Elizabeth Furnival
Parents: Thomas Furnival (76B01) and Mary Cadman
Born: 1798
Baptised: 23 December 1798 (Moreton Say?)

83B01   Elizabeth Furnival
Grandparents: William Furnival (75B01) and Hannah Barker
Parents: Daniel Furnival (79B01) and Ann Heywood
Born 1838
Married George Taylor on 16 February 1865 at the age of 27

85B01   Elizabeth Ann Furnival
Great-Grandparents: William Furnival (75B01) and Hannah Barker
Grandparents: Daniel Furnival (79B01) and Ann Heywood
Parents: Stephen Furnival (82B01) and Fanny Bourne
Born:1857 and died the same year on 11 November.

Elizabeth Furnival see Annie Elizabeth Furnival (86B01)

Ellen, Ellina, or Ellinor Furnival

74B01   Ellina Furnival
Parents: William Furnival (70M01) and Cassandra Wright
Born: 1744
Baptised at Moreton Say 27 March 1744

76B01   Ellinor Furnival
Grandparents: William Furnival (70M01) and Cassandra Wright
Parents: John Furnival (73B01) and Mary
Born: 1767
Baptised: 8 September 1767 at Moreton Say

Ellen Furnival see Eliza Ellen Furnival (78B02)

82B01   Ellen Furnival
Grandparents: William Furnival (75B01) and Hannah Barker
Parents: William Furnival (78B03) and Sarah Tweed
Born 1821
According to the Roy Furnival archive

85B01   Ellen Furnival
Great-Grandparents: William Furnival (75B01) and Hannah Barker
Grandparents: William Furnival (78B03) and Sarah Tweed
Parents: Daniel Furnival (81B01) and Sarah Ridgway
Born: 1858
Baptised 10 October 1858 at Norton-in-Hales

Emily Furnival

Emily Furnival see Marjorie Emily Furnival (85E01)

Eva Furnival

86M01   Eva Mary Furnival
Great-Grandparents: William Furnival (75B01) and Hannah Barker
Grandparents: Daniel Furnival (79B01) and Ann Heywood
Parents: Edward Furnival (84B01) and Helen Hordley
She married J F Moss in 1900 and had two children.

Fanny Furnival

86B01   Fanny Eliza Furnival
Great-Grandparents: William Furnival (75B01) and Hannah Barker
Grandparents: Daniel Furnival (79B01) and Ann Heywood
Parents: Stephen Furnival (82B01) and Fanny Bourne
Born: 1864
Married The Reverend Beeston

88B01   Fanny Valentine Furnival
Great-Great-Grandparents: William Furnival (75B01) and Hannah Barker
Great-Grandparents: Daniel Furnival (79B01) and Ann Heywood
Grandparents: Stephen Furnival (82B01) and Fanny Bourne
Parents: John Stephen Furnival (85B01) and May Bourne
Born 1880
Baptised 19 February 1880 in Norton-in-Hales

Frederick Furnival

86B01   Frederick William Furnival
Great-Grandparents: William Furnival (75B01) and Hannah Barker
Grandparents: Daniel Furnival (79B01) and Ann Heywood
Parents: Stephen Furnival (82B01) and Fanny Bourne
Born: 8 May 1868
Married Edith Eardley in 1898
Their son John Stephen Furnival was born on Christmas Day 1899 but his genealogy is withheld from these notes because of the Mercianotes policy not to publish details of people born after 1900.

88E01   Fred Stephen Furnival
Great-Great-Grandparents: William Furnival (75B01) and Hannah Barker
Great-Grandparents: Daniel Furnival (79B01) and Ann Heywood
Grandparents: Stephen Furnival (82B01) and Fanny Bourne
Parents: John Stephen Furnival (85B01) and May Bourne

Hannah Furnival

83B01   Hannah Eliza Furnival
Grandparents: William Furnival (75B01) and Hannah Barker
Parents: Daniel Furnival (79B01) and Ann Heywood
Born 1836/7
Married William Wigglesworth 28 April 1864 at the age of 28.

Harold Furnival

88E01   Harold Studley Furnival
Great-Great-Grandparents: William Furnival (75B01) and Hannah Barker
Great-Grandparents: Daniel Furnival (79B01) and Ann Heywood
Grandparents: Stephen Furnival (82B01) and Fanny Bourne
Parents: John Stephen Furnival (85B01) and May Bourne

Henry Furnival

82B01   Henry Furnival
Grandparents: William Furnival (75B01) and Hannah Barker
Parents: William Furnival (78B03) and Sarah Tweed
Born 1825 (twin)
According to the Roy Furnival archive

84B01   Henry Furnival
Grandparents: William Furnival (75B01) and Hannah Barker
Parents: Daniel Furnival (79B01) and Ann Heywood
Born 1844
married in 1868? at Newcastle?, Staffs.

Henry Furnival see William Henry Furnival (84B01)
Henry Furnival see Edwin Henry Furnival (85B01)

85B02   Henry Furnival
Great-Grandparents: William Furnival (75B01) and Hannah Barker
Grandparents: William Furnival (78B03) and Sarah Tweed
Parents: Daniel Furnival (81B01) and Sarah Ridgway
Born: 1857
Baptised 18 January 1857 at Norton-in-Hales.

Hurdley Furnival

86E01   Hurdley Furnival
Great-Grandparents: William Furnival (75B01) and Hannah Barker
Grandparents: Daniel Furnival (79B01) and Ann Heywood
Parents: Edward Furnival (84B01) and Helen Hordley
Married Elsie.
They had a son Ted (Edward) (88E01)

James Furnival

81B01   James Furnival
Parents: William Furnival (78M01) and Elizabeth
Born: 1811
Baptised 17 March 1811 in Mucklestone.

82B01   James Furnival
Grandparents: William Furnival (75B01) and Hannah Barker
Parents: Daniel Furnival (79B01) and Ann Heywood
Born 1826

Died 1849 at Napley Heath aged 23 and was buried at Mucklestone on 31 August 1849
James lived at Knighton

Jane Furnival

80B01   Jane Furnival
Parents: Thomas Furnival (76B01) and Mary Cadman
Born: 1803
Baptised: 20 February 1803 (Moreton Say?)

John or Jonathan Furnival

69M01   John Furnifar Of Aston
He had a son Thomas who was buried at Mucklestone on 29 March 1780. Assuming Thomas died at 70, and John was 20 when Thomas was born, Then John would be born circa 1690.
Thomas (71D01) was buried at Mucklestone on 29 March 1780.

66E01   John Furwood of Knighton
Had a son Charles Furwood (68D01) who was Buried at Mucklestone 1 Sept 1757. Assuming Charles was 70 when he died, and that John was 20 when Charles was born. John would be born circa 1680.
This is included in this study in case 'Furwood' is a miss spelling of 'Furnival'

72B01   Jonathan Furnival
Parents: William Furnival (70M01) and Cassandra Wright
Born 1724
Baptised at Moreton Say 1 May 1724

73B01   John Furnival
Parents: William Furnival (70M01) and Cassandra Wright
Born: 1733
Baptised at Moreton Say 16 February 1733
Married Mary and had the following children
John (75B01) born: 1759
Mary (76B01) born: 1760
Daniel (76B01) born: 1764
Ellinor (76B01) born: 1767

75B01   John Furnival
Grandparents: William Furnival (70M01) and Cassandra Wright
Parents: John Furnival (73B01) and Mary
Born: 1759
Baptised: 22 April 1759 at Moreton Say
Married Sarah Adams 29 November 1794

78B01   John Furnival
Parents: William Furnival (75B01) and
Hannah Barker
Born 1783
Baptised at Mucklestone 13 August 1783
Married 29 June 1806 at Market Drayton
Died 1850 (The Roy Furnival Archive
records the death as 1854)

81B01   John Furnival
Parents: William Furnival (78M01) and
Elizabeth
Born: 1813
Baptised 8 August 1813 in Mucklestone.
He was a labourer in Knighton

81B02   John Furnival
Grandparents: William Furnival (75B01)
and Hannah Barker
Parents: William Furnival (78B03) and
Sarah Tweed
Born 1816
Baptised in Mucklestone 14 January 1816
He was at Napley Heath in 1861 and later
became a farmer at Winnington

82B01   John Furnival
Grandparents: William Furnival (75B01)
and Hannah Barker
Parents: Daniel Furnival (79B01) and
Ann Heywood
Born 1820
Baptised 13 August 1820
Died 1845
He was a bookseller in Market Drayton.
He had a daughter who was born after
1845 who was mentioned in Daniel's
Will and also in John's Will.

82B02   John Furnival of Market Drayton
Born 1821
Buried at Mucklestone March 1845 aged 24.

83B01   John Furnival
Son of Thomas Furnival (80B01) and Eliza
Born: 1839

84B01   John Daniel Furnival
Grandparents: William Furnival (75B01)
and Hannah Barker
Parents: Daniel Furnival (79B01) and
Ann Heywood
Born 1846
John was a chemist.
He married his first wife, Mary Caroline
(Wareham?) Of Newcastle in 1872
and his second wife Sarah Jane Barlow of
Stoke on Trent, sometime later.
He might have had a son called Roy
(86B01)
John died in 1928

85B01   John Stephen Furnival
Great-Grandparents: William Furnival
(75B01) and Hannah Barker
Grandparents: Daniel Furnival (79B01)
and Ann Heywood
Parents: Stephen Furnival (82B01) and
Fanny Bourne
Born: 26 September 1858
Buried 17 December 1950 aged 92 at
Mucklestone
Married May Bourne and had the follow-
ing children.
Fanny Valentine (88B01) born: 1880
Stephen (88E01)
Tom (88E01)
S. W.
Fred Stephen (88E01)
Edwin Bourne (88E01)
Harold Studley (88E01)
Doris May (88E01)

89B01   John William Furnival
Great-Great-Grandparents: William Fur-
nival (75B01) and Hannah Barker
Great-Grandparents: William Furnival
(78B03) and Sarah Tweed
Grandparents: Thomas Furnival (82M01)
spouse not known
Parents: William Henry Furnival (84B01)
spouse not known
Born: 1895
He was a farmer and stonemason.
He married Esther Ann Oakley. They had
a son born after 1900
John died in 1955

Joseph Furnival

80B01   Joseph Furnival
Parents: William Furnival (78M01) and
Elizabeth
Born: 1808
Baptised 11 December 1808 in Muckle-
stone.

Marjory, Marjorie or Margery Furnival

Marjory Furnival see Ann Majory Furnival (83B01)

86E02   Margery Furnival
Great-Grandparents: William Furnival
(75B01) and Hannah Barker
Grandparents: Daniel Furnival (79B01)
and Ann Heywood
Parents: Edward Furnival (84B01) and
Helen Hordley

19

85E01   Marjorie Emily Furnival

According to the Roy Furnival Archive:
Great-Grandparents: William Furnival
(75B01) and Hannah Barker
Grandparents: Daniel Furnival (79B01)
and Ann Heywood
Parents: Stephen Furnival (82B01) and
Fanny Bourne
She married Thomas Bourne of Napley.

Martha Furnival

73B01   Martha Furnival

Parents: William Furnival (70M01) and
Cassandra Wright
Born: 1730
Baptised at Moreton Say 6 March 1730
She must have died in infancy, because
she had a sister also called Martha - see
below.

73B02   Martha Furnival

Parents: William Furnival (70M01) and
Cassandra Wright
Born: 1736
Baptised at Moreton Say 3 Jan 1736

75B01   Martha Furnival

Grandparents: William Furnival (70M01)
and Cassandra Wright
Parents: William Furnival (72B01) and
Elizabeth Rigg
Born 1755

79B01   Martha Furnival

Parents: William Furnival (75B01) and
Hannah Barker
Born 1796 and was baptised at Muckle-
stone 5 Jan 1796
.Married John Bartlam at Mucklestone 30
September 1816

80B01   Martha Furnival

Parents: Thomas Furnival (76B01) and
Mary Cadman
Born: 1807
Baptised: 19 July 1807 (Moreton Say?)

83B01   Martha Furnival

Grandparents: William Furnival (75B01)
and Hannah Barker
Parents: Daniel Furnival (79B01) and
Ann Heywood
Born 1833
She married Daniel Eardley sometime
after 1851.
They moved to Sheffield and had a child
J.F. Eardley

Martha Furnival see Alice Martha Furnival (86B01)

Mary Furnival

73B01   Mary Furnival

Parents: William Furnival (70M01) and
Cassandra Wright
Born: 1738
Baptised at Moreton Say 5 August 1738
Buried at Moreton Say 24 August 1745
aged 7 years

75B01   Mary Furnival

Grandparents: William Furnival (70M01)
and Cassandra Wright
Parents: William Furnival (72B01) and
Elizabeth Rigg
Born 1758

76B01   Mary Furnival

Grandparents: William Furnival (70M01)
and Cassandra Wright
Parents: John Furnival (73B01) and Mary
Born: 1760
Baptised: 26 December 1760 at Moreton
Say

80B01   Mary Furnival

Parents: Thomas Furnival (76B01) and
Mary Cadman
Born: 1801
Baptised: 15 February 1801 (Moreton
Say?)

81B01   Mary Furnival

Parents: William Furnival (78M01) and
Elizabeth
Born: 1816
Baptised 18 August 1816 in Mucklestone.

82B01   Mary Furnival

Grandparents: William Furnival (75B01)
and Hannah Barker
Parents: William Furnival (78B03) and
Sarah Tweed
Born 1823
According to the Roy Furnival archive

83B01   Mary Furnival

Grandparents: William Furnival (75B01)
and Hannah Barker
Parents: Daniel Furnival (79B01) and
Ann Heywood
Born 1839
Died 1844 at Napley Heath aged 5 and
was buried at Mucklestone 13 December
1844

84B01   Mary Anne Furnival of Knighton
Born 1840
Buried at Mucklestone 18 February 1842
aged 2.

84B02   Mary Furnival
Grandparents: Thomas Furnival (76B01)
and Mary Cadman
Parents: Thomas Furnival (80B01) and
Eliza
Born: 1841

Mary Furnival see Eva Mary Furnival (86M01)
Mary Furnival see Edith Mary Furnival (87B01)
May Furnival see Doris May Furnival (88E01)

Minnie Furnival

87B01   Minnie Susan Furnival
Great-Grandparents: William Furnival
(75B01) and Hannah Barker
Grandparents: Daniel Furnival (79B01)
and Ann Heywood
Parents: Stephen Furnival (82B01) and
Fanny Bourne
Born: 1873
Married Martin Bourne

Roy Furnival

86B01   Roy Furnival
The son of John Daniel Furnival (84B01).
If Roy was born when John Daniel was
20, then Roy would be born circa 1860.
This record is subject to confirmation.

Sarah Furnival

80B01   Sarah Furnival
Parents: Thomas Furnival (76B01) and
Mary Cadman
Born: 1809
Baptised: 23 July 1809 (Moreton Say?)

82E01   Sarah Furnival
Grandparents: William Furnival (75B01)
and Hannah Barker
Parents: William Furnival (78B03) and
Sarah Tweed
According to the Roy Furnival archive

84B01   Sarah Furnival of Napley Heath
Grandparents: William Furnival (75B01)
and Hannah Barker
Parents: Daniel Furnival (79B01) and
Ann Heywood
Born 1842
Buried at Mucklestone 18 April 1842
aged 2 months

Stephen Furnival

82B01   Stephen Furnival
Grandparents: William Furnival (75B01)
and Hannah Barker
Parents: Daniel Furnival (79B01) and
Ann Heywood
Born 1822
Married Fanny Bourne April 1854 (when
he was 32)
Edwin Henry (85B01) born: 1855
Elizabeth Ann (85B01) born:1857
John Stephen (85B01) born: 1858
Annie Elizabeth (86B01) born: 1861
Fanny Eliza (86B01) born: 1864
Alice Martha (86B01) born: 1866
Frederick William (86B01) born: 1868
Edith Mary (87B01) born: 1871
Minnie Susan (87B01) born: 1873
Marjorie Emily (according to Roy Furni-
val Archive)
Died 1883 (aged 61) and
buried at Mucklestone 29 July 1883.

Stephen Furnival see John Stephen Furnival (85B01)
Stephen Furnival see Fred Stephen Furnival (88E01)

88E01   Stephen Furnival
Great-Great-Grandparents: William Furnival (75B01) and Hannah Barker
Great-Grandparents: Daniel Furnival
(79B01) and Ann Heywood
Grandparents: Stephen Furnival (82B01)
and Fanny Bourne
Parents: John Stephen Furnival (85B01)
and May Bourne

Studley Furnival

Studley Furnival see Harold Studley Furnival (88E01)

Susan Furnival

Susan Furnival see Minnie Susan Furnival (87B01)

Thomas Furnival

71D01   Thomas Furnifar of Aston
He was the son of John Furnifar (69M01)
Thomas was buried at Mucklestone on 29
March 1780.
Assuming Thomas died at 70, he would
be born circa 1710.

74B01   Thomas Furnival
Parents: William Furnival (70M01) and
Cassandra Wright
Born: 1741
Baptised at Moreton Say 1 January 1741
Married Hanna Evans at Moreton Say on
29 December 1772 he was 31.

21

76B01   Thomas Furnival
Born: 1768
Baptised 17 July 1768 (Moreton Say?)
Married Mary Cadman 13 April 1795
  (Moreton Say?)
Children:
  Ann (79B02) born: 1795
  Elizabeth (79B01)born: 1798
  Mary (80B01) born: 1801
  Jane (80B01) born: 1803
  Thomas (80B01) born: 1805
  Martha (80B01) born: 1807
  Sarah (80B01) born: 1809
  William (81B02) born: 1812

80B01   Thomas Furnival
Parents: Thomas Furnival (76B01) and
  Mary Cadman
Born: 1805
Baptised: 22 July 1805 (Moreton Say?)
He was a blacksmith
Married Eliza, a dressmaker who was
  born in 1811
Children:
  Thomas (83B01) born: 1831
  Eliza (83B01) born: 1833
  William (83B02) born: 1837
  John (83B01) born: 1839
  Mary (84B02) born: 1841

82M01   Thomas Furnival
Grandparents: William Furnival (75B01)
  and Hannah Barker
Parents: William Furnival (78B03) and
  Sarah Tweed
According to the Roy Furnival archive
Thomas was a travelling preacher from
1815 onwards.
Details of his marriage are not available
but he had one son
  William Henry (84B01) born 1841.
He died a widower in 1851

83B01   Thomas Furnival
Grandparents: Thomas Furnival (76B01)
  and Mary Cadman
Parents: Thomas Furnival (80B01) and
  Eliza
Born: 1831

88E01   Tom B Furnival
Great-Great-Grandparents: William Furnival (75B01) and Hannah Barker
Great-Grandparents: Daniel Furnival
  (79B01) and Ann Heywood
Grandparents: Stephen Furnival (82B01)
  and Fanny Bourne
Parents: John Stephen Furnival (85B01)
  and May Bourne

Valentine Furnival

*Valentine Furnival see Fanny Valentine Furnival
(88B01)*

William Furnival

70M01   William Furnival
Married Cassandra Wright 6 January
  1723/4 at Moreton Say
Children:
  Jonathan (72B01) born: 1724
  William (72B01) born: 1726
  Martha (73B01) born: 1730
  John (73B01) born: 1733
  Martha (73B02) born: 1736
  Mary (73B01) born: 1738
  Thomas (74B01) born: 1741
  Ellina (74B01) born: 1744
There is a record of William Furnival be-
ing buried at Morton Say on 3rd Septem-
ber 1782. This would make him at least
79. However, the record could refer to
his son.

72B01   William Furnival
Parents: William Furnival (70M01) and
  Cassandra Wright
Born: 1726
Baptised at Moreton Say 29 September
  1726
He married Elizabeth Rigg on 7 January
  1754
Martha (75B01) born: 1755
Mary (75B01) born: 1758
William (76B01) born: 1764
There is a record of William Furnival be-
ing buried at Morton Say on 3rd Septem-
ber 1782. This would make him 56.
However, the record could refer to his
father.

75B01   William Furnival
of Napley Heath in the parish of Muckle-
stone.
Born 1759
Married Hannah Barker also of Muckle-
stone 9 December 1782
Children:
  William died 1840 and was buried in
  Mucklestone 7 December 1840
  John (78B01) born: 1783
  Elizabeth (78B01) born: 1785
  William (78B03) born: 1789
  Eliza Ellen (78B02) born: 1787
  Daniel (79B01) born: 1792
  Martha (79B01) born: 1796

76B01   William Furnival
Grandparents: William Furnival (70M01)
and Cassandra Wright
Parents: William Furnival (72B01) and
Elizabeth Rigg
Born 1764
Married Eleanor Parker 17 December
1789

78M01   William Furnival of Knighton
Born sometime between 1740 and 1780
Assuming Joseph was born when William
was 20, he would have been born circa
1780.
Assuming Ann was born when William
was 60, he would have been born circa
1740.
Married Elizabeth
Children:
Joseph (80B01) born: 1808
James(81B01) born: 1811
John (81B01) born: 1813
Mary (81B01) born: 1816
Ann (81B01) born: 1818

78B02   William Furnival of Dorrington
Born 1784
Buried at Mucklestone 11 Feb 1831 aged
47.

78B03   William Furnival
According to the Roy Furnival archive:-
Parents: William Furnival (75B01) and
Hannah Barker
Born 1789
He was at Napley Heath when William
(82B02) died.
Married Sarah Tweed circa 1815
Died 1854
Children:
John (81B02) born: 1816
Daniel (81B01) born: 1817
William (81B01) born: 1819
Thomas (82M01)
Sarah (82E01)
Ellen (82B01) born: 1821
Mary (82B01) born: 1823
William (82B02) born: 1825 (twin)
Henry (82B01) born: 1825 (twin)

81B01   William Furnival
Grandparents: William Furnival (75B01)
and Hannah Barker
Parents: William Furnival (78B03) and
Sarah Tweed
Born 1819
Baptised 12 December 1819 and must
have died before 1825 when the twins
Henry (82B01) and William (82B01)
were born.
He probably died at birth

81B02   William Furnival
Parents: Thomas Furnival (76B01) and
Mary Cadman
Born: 1812
Baptised: 19 January 1812 Moreton Say

82B01   William Furnival of Winnington Forge
Born 1820
Buried at Mucklestone 13 July 1822 aged
2 years 9 months.

82B02   William Furnival of Napley Heath
Grandparents: William Furnival (75B01)
and Hannah Barker
Parents: William Furnival (78B03) and
Sarah Tweed
Born 1825 (twin)
Buried at Mucklestone 9 December 1825
aged 2 weeks
Information from Roy Furnival Archive
and Mucklestone Parish Register.

83B01   William Furnival
Grandparents: William Furnival
(75B01) and Hannah Barker
Parents: Daniel Furnival (79B01) and
Ann Heywood
Born 1835
He is recorded as being unmarried in 1851

83B02   William Furnival
Grandparents: Thomas Furnival (76B01)
and Mary Cadman
Parents: Thomas Furnival (80B01) and
Eliza
Born: 1837

84B01   William Henry Furnival
Great-Grandparents: William Furnival
(75B01) and Hannah Barker
Grandparents: William Furnival (78B03)
and Sarah Tweed
Parents: Thomas Furnival (82M01)
spouse not known
Born 1841
Died: 1907
He was a farmer and built Napley Villa
Children:
John William (89B01) born: 1895

William Furnival see Frederick William Furnival (86B01)

86E04   William 'Billy' Furnival
Great-Grandparents: William Furnival
(75B01) and Hannah Barker
Grandparents: Daniel Furnival (79B01)
and Ann Heywood
Parents: Edward Furnival (84B01) and
Helen Hordley
Married Daisy

William Furnival see John William Furnival (89B01)

The In-Laws of the Furnivals

Adams
Sarah Adams = John Furnival (75B01)

Barker
Hannah Barker of the parish of Mucklestone married William Furnival (75B01). She was born in 1750, died at the age of 80 and was buried at Mucklestone on 7 February 1830.

Barlow
Sarah Jane Barlow = John Daniel Furnival (84B01)

Bartlam
John Bartlam = Martha Furnival (79B01)

Beeston
The Reverend Beeston = Fanny Eliza Furnival (86B01)

Bourne
Fanny Bourne married Stephen Furnival (82B01). Born in 1826 (Bapt 28 Jan 1826) the daughter of Samuel Bourne of Studby, she was buried on 20 March 1913.

Martin Bourne = Minnie Susan Furnival (87B01)

May Bourne married John Stephen Furnival (85B01). Born 1 May 1862 the daughter of John Borne of Arbour Farm and Studley Farm, she was buried on 5 July 1921 aged 59.

J E Bourne married Alice Martha Furnival (86B01)

Thomas Bourne of Napley = Marjorie Emily Furnival (85E01)

Cadman
Mary Cadman = Thomas Furnival (76B01)

Cook
Harry Cook = Edith Mary Furnival (87B01)

Eardley
Edith Eardley married Frederick William Furnival (86B01) in 1898. She was born on 13 November 1866 and was buried on 3 Feb 1943 aged 77 years.

Daniel Eardley married Martha Furnival (83B01)

Evans
Hanna Evans married Thomas Furnival (74B01)

Highfield
Ann Highfield married Daniel Furnival (79B01). Ann was the daughter of John and Margery of Knighton

Heywood
Ann Heywood married Daniel Furnival (79B01). Ann Heywood of Napley Farm was born in 1799 and died in December 1846

Hordley
Helen Hordley married Edward Furnival (84B01)

Mate
William Mate married Ann Margery Furnival (83B01) 13 May 1859. He was the son of William Mate, a farmer of Norton in Hales.

Meakin
Elizabeth ('Lizzie') Meakin married Edwin Henry Furnival (85B01). Elizabeth was the daughter of William Meakin of Lea Head. She lived at Bellaport Park Farm, then, according to the 1896 edition of Kelly's Directory, 1896 at Tudley Farm. Lizzie was buried in Norton-in-Hales Cemetary 6 December 1912

Moss J F Moss married Eva Mary Furnival (86M01)

Parker Eleanor Parker married William Furnival (76B01)17 December 1789

Oakley Esther Ann Oakley married John William Furnival (89B01)

Ridgway Sarah Ridgway, daughter of Joseph Ridgway, married Daniel Furnival (81B01)

Rigg Elizabeth Rigg married William Furnival (72B01)

Rodenhurst William Rodenhurst married Annie Elizabeth Furnival (86B01)

Spragg John Spragg of Ridgewardine married Ann Furnival (79B02). He was born 1799 and was recorded in the census of 1851 as being 52 years old.

Taylor George Taylor married Elizabeth Furnival (83B01) on 16 February 1865. He was a wine merchant in Wigglesworth, Manchester

Tweed Sarah Tweed married William Furnival (78B03)

Wigglesworth William Wigglesworth married Hannah Eliza Furnival (83B01) 28 April 1864. He was a Manchester solicitor

Wright Cassandra Wright married William Furnival (70M01)

Nancy Lindop's Notes

on
The Jones Family
Of Woore

Compiled by Geoffrey H. Lindop

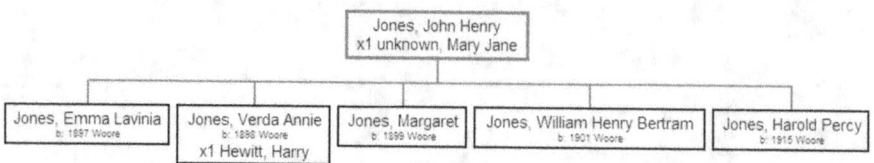

The following information has been taken from various editions of the Woore Parish Magazine.

John Henry and Mary Jane Jones had the following children:

Emma Lavinia was baptised 21 February 1897

Verda Annie Jones was baptised on 17 July 1898 and married Harry Hewitt on 20 December 1914.

Margaret Jones was baptised on 6 August 1899.

William Henry Bertram Jones was baptised on 17 November 1901.

Wilfred John Jones married Elizabeth Wright at Woore on 6th December 1909.

Their daughter, Mary Jane was baptised on 14th August 1910.

Nancy Lindop's Additional Research

Joseph and Jane Jones of Gravenhunger Moss had two children: Arthur baptised on 20th February 1898 and Alic baptised on 13 September 1899.

Frederick Jones married Elizabeth DEELEY and lived at the School House, Woore. Their daughter Marion was baptised on 17 July 1898.

John Henry and Mary Jane JONES also had a daughter Doris Elizabeth baptised on 15 July 1906 and their son Harold Percy was baptised on 18 April 1915.

The following information has been taken from directories.

John Henry Jones was a butcher in Woore in 1905 (1)

John Henry Jones was a butcher in Woore in 1913 (2)

Thomas Jones lived at the Square in Woore in 1913 (2)

John Jones was a Saddler at the Square and Nantwich Road, Woore in 1933 (2)

Mrs Harriette E. Jones was the postmistress at Woore in 1913 (2)

Mrs Harriet Eliz. Jones had a boot and shoe shop in Woore in 1937 (1)

Mrs Harriette E. Jones was the postmistress at Woore in 1940 (2)

John Jones was a Saddler at the Square and Natwich Road, Woore in 1940 (2)

Mrs Harriet Eliz. Jones had a boot and shoe shop and was the Postmistress in Woore in 1941 (1)

John Jones was a Saddler in Woore in 1941 (1)

Reference

Please refer to the appropriate year of the following:

1. Kelly's Directory

2. Advertiser Almanack and Directory

The following information has been taken from the Churchyard.

IN LOVING MEMORY OF
HARRIET ELIZABETH JONES
WHO DIED JUNE 15TH 1952
AGED 62 YEARS
ALSO HER HUSBAND
JOHN JONES
WHO DIED JULY 31ST 1962
AGED 71 YEARS

The following information has been taken from the War Memorial in the Churchyard :

IN EVER
GRATEFUL
MEMORY OF THOSE WHO
GAVE THEIR
LIVES IN THE
GREAT WAR
1914-1918
AND
ESPECIALLY
OF THE MEN
OF THIS
PARISH HERE
RECORDED

JOSEPH COLLIN BROWN L Cpl
RICHARD ALLEN CRABTREE Pte
THOMAS DALE Pte
ALBERT LEONARD FOXLEY Snr
CLAUDE WILLIAM GRIFFIN Pte
ALBERT GROOM Pte
ABNER JAMES Pte
ARTHUR JONES Pte
JOSEPH JONES Pte
HORACE HARRY JONES Pte
FREDERICK LEIGHTON Pte
GEORGE Wm LIGHTFOOT Pte
PERCY MELLOR 2nd Lt
THOMAS MINSHULL Pte

GORDON MOUNTFORD 2nd Lt
WILLIAM MORREY Pte
WILLIAM NAGGINGTON Pie
RALPH TWIST SNARE Pte
THOMAS SMITH Pte
ARTHUR TAYLOR Pte
JAMES WILLIAM TITLEY Pte
JOHN WALLACE Pte
WILLIAM WESTON Cpl

1939-1945
JAMES DOYLE Lt Col
LESLIE JONES Pte

The Shuker Family
of
North Shropshire

Compiled by Geoffrey and Nancy Lindop

MERCIANOTES

This booklet is compiled from transcripts of printed parish registers published by the Shropshire Parish Register Society. The original registers were handwritten by individuals and therefore their spelling of surnames was often erratic. Some entries were originally written in Latin. Errors are prone to creep in due to spelling, translation, and interpretation of handwriting. The diligent researcher is always advised to consult original documents, yet this advise of sometimes impractical. Wherever such errors are likely to occur the following conventions are observed throughout this book.

{words in curly brackets}	are exactly as written in the reference document cited at the end of each section. Sometimes these words are clearly in error.
[words in square brackets]	are those of the Editor. These may be assumptions or clarifications to a passage.
Words outside brackets	are sentences derived from the cited sources and expressed in a logical order in modern English.

Adderley

No members found in this parish

Period researched: Baptisms 1692-1812 Marriages 1692-1812 Burials 1692-1812
Reference: Adderley Parish Register in Lichfield Volume 4

Alberbury

1572 Apr. 8   Andrews Suker was buried
1619 May 30   William Cowper from Ponsonby and Johanna Suker were married. {Willimus Cowper, parish de Ponsburie et Johanna Suker de eode}
1633 Apr. 14   Elizabeth daughter of George and Johanne Suker from Prees was buried. {Elizabetha, f. Georgii et Johanne Suker, de Preece}

Albrighton nr Shrewsbury

No members found in this parish.

Period researched: Baptisms 1649-1812 Marriages 1649-1812 Burials 1649-1812
Reference: Albrighton Parish Register in Lichfield Volume 1

Astley

No members found in this parish.

Period researched: Baptisms 1695-1815 Marriages 1754-1812 Burials 1695-1815
Reference: Astley Parish Register in Lichfield Volume 4 part 1

Atcham

No members found in this parish.

Period researched: Baptisms 1621-1812Marriages 1621-1837Burials 1621-1812
Reference: Atcham Parish Register in Lichfield Vol 14 Part 2

Battlefield

1730 Dec. 23   Mr. William Birchall and Mrs. Joyce Sucar both of the Parish of
Drayton were married.

Period researched: Baptisms 1663-1812 Marriages 1663-1812 Burials 1663-1812
Reference: Battlefield Parish Register in Lichfield Volume 1

Berrington

No members found in this parish.

Period researched: Baptisms 1560-1812 Marriages 1561-1837 Burials 1560-1812
Reference: Berrington Parish Register in Lichfield Volume 14 part 4

Clive

1636   William Sugar became the Incumbent of Clive in 1636. He was
also Curate of Grinshill and Broughton. He was buried at
Broughton 17 March 1675.

Period researched: Baptisms 1676-1812 Marriages 1676-1812 Burials 1676-1812
Reference: Clive Parish Register in Lichfield Volume 8 part 2

Condover

No members found in this parish.

Period researched: Baptisms 1570-1812 Marriages 1570-1812 Burials 1570-1812
Reference: Condover Parish Register in Lichfield Volume 6 Part 1

Edstaston

No members found in this parish.

Period researched: Baptisms 1713-1812 Marriages 1731-1753 Burials 1712-1812
Reference: Edstaston Parish Register in Lichfield Volume 10

Fitz

1746 Feb. 8   Richard Shuker parish of St. Chadds, and Eliz. Parr, of Fitz
(servants) were married.

1747 Dec. 31   Elizabeth, daughter of Richard and Elizabeth Shuker, of Mitton
was baptised.

Period researched: Baptisms 1559-1812 Marriages 1559-1812 Burials 1559-1812
Reference: Fitz Parish Register in Lichfield Volume 4

Great Ness

1748 Dec. 22	Edward Shuker and Catherine Jones were married
1749 Nov. 6	Mary, daughter of Edward and Catharine Shukar, was baptised.
1750 Sept.	Edward Shukar signed the register as a Churchwarden.

1752, Jan. 6	Anne, daughter of Edw. and Catherine Shukar, was baptised.
1754 July 18	Samuel, son of Edw. and Catharine Shukar, was baptised.
1756 April 5	Edward Shukar, {A mortuary paid}, was buried.

1756 Feb. 5	Edward, son of John and Elizabeth Shukar, was baptised.
1756 July 16	Ric. Cooper, a servant and Catherine Shuker a widow were married by licence. The wedding was witnessed by John Thomas, and Eliz. Trustrem.

1757 Dec. 31	John Shuker, a widower. of Battlefield and Elizabeth Trustrem, a spinster [presumably of Great Ness], were married by licence. The wedding was witnessed by Ric. Nunnerley and Eliz. Nunnerley.

1760 Apr. 19	Thomas, son of John and Elizabeth Shukar, was baptised.
1762 June 13	Richard, son of John and Elizabeth Shukar, was baptised.
1763 Mar. 16	John Shuker was buried.

1763, July 11	Richard Shuker, an infant, was buried.
1770 Aug. 8	Robert Matthews, bachelor, and Mary Shuker, spinster, were married by licence. The wedding was witnessed by Thos. Rye, and Ann Shuker.

1778, Feb. 5	John Jones, bachelor, and Anne Shuker, spinster were married, [both were presumably from this parish]. The wedding was witnessed by Jn. Jones, and Eliz. Jones.

1788 Sep. 28	Catherine, daughter of Robert Matthews of the Lane, by Mary, his wife formerly Mary Shuker. Catherine was born Sep. 6 and baptised on Sep 28. Robert Matthews was a shoemaker.

Period researched: Baptisms 1589-1864 Marriages 1589-1864 Burials 1589-1864
Reference: Great Ness Parish Register in Lichfield Volume 20

Grinshill

No members of the family are recorded in this parish, except the rather tenuous reference of William Sugar as noted in the Clive section.

Period researched: Baptisms 1592-1812 Marriages 1592-1812 Burials 1592-1812
Reference: Grinshill Parish Register in Lichfield Volume 2

Harley

No members found in this parish.

Period researched: 1590-1812
Reference: Harley Parish Register in Lichfield Volume 2

High Ercall

1610 April 4	Richard, son of Abraham and Elizabeth Suker of Rodon, was baptised.
1632 June 17	Marie, daughter of Richard and Margret Suker of Haughton, was baptised.
1634 Feb. 9	Abraham, son of Richard and Margret Suker of Haughton, was baptised.
1636 Sep. 4	Richard, son of Richard and {Margrete} Suker of Haughton, was baptised.
1636 Nov. 20	Ric. Suker, of Haugton, an {infante}, was buried.
1638 Jan. 28	Margret, daughter of Richard and Margret Suker of Haughton, was baptised.
1641 Apr. 27	Elizabeth, daughter of Richard and {Margrett} Suker of Haughton, was baptised.
1644 Feb. 12	Ursula, daughter of Richard and Margret Suker of Haughton, was baptised.
1648 Feb. 10	George, son of Richard and {Margaret} Suker of Haughton, was baptised.
1657, Aug. 14	Elizabeth, wife of Abraham Suker of Haughton, was buried.
1661 Jan. 30	Abraham Suker, {of Haughton, who was of very old age} {de Haughton, valde annosus}, was buried.
1674 Sept. 22	Margaret wife of Richard Sugar of Haughton, was buried. {Margaretae, uxor Richardi Sugar, de Haughton}
1676 Mar. 9	Humphrey, son of Humphrey and Elizabeth Suker of Painton, was baptised. {Humfredus, f, Humfredi Suker de Painton, et Elizabethae}
1689 Mar. 10	George, son of Richard Shuker of Haughton, was buried. {Georgius, f. Richardi Shuker, de Haughton}
1692 Nov. 18	Richard Sukar of Haughton was buried. {Richardus Sukar, de Haughton}
1800 May 25	John, son of Thomas Shuker of Ellerdine Heath, was baptised
1802 Aug. 29	Mary, daughter of Thomas Shuker of Ellerdine Heath, was baptised.

1803, Mar. 13   Elizabeth, daughter of William Shuker of Ellerdine Heath, was baptised.

1803 Nov. 24   M. Shuker and Joseph Matthews witnessed the wedding of Thomas Cooper and Mary Matthews.

1804 July 22   Sarah, daughter of Thomas Shuker of Ellerdine, was baptised.

1811 Sep. 30   Thomas Higginson and Elizabeth Shuker were married. The wedding was witnessed by Thomas Williams and Emma Humphries.

1822 Nov. 16   John Shuker, of the parish of Wellington, and Elizabeth Hodgkiss [of this parish], were married. The wedding was witnessed by Thos. Hodgkiss and Elizabeth Shuker.

1824 Nov. 22   William Shuker and Mary Worrall were married. The wedding was witnessed by Edward Worrall and Eleanor Jones.

1827 Dec. 31   Thomas Wedge and Elizabeth Shuker were married with consent of parents. The wedding was witnessed by Joseph Wedge and Mary Shuker.

Period researched: Baptisms 1585-1651 Marriages 1585-1651 Burials 1585-1651
Reference: High Ercall Parish Register in Lichfield Volume 20 Part 3

Hodnet

1663 Aug. 10   Thomas Suker and Elizabeth Blackway were married
1664 May 19   Anne, daughter to Thomas and Elizabeth Suker, was baptised
1666 Aug. 16   Thomas, son to Thomas and Elizabeth Suker, was baptised

1667 May 1   Thomas Suker was buried. [There is an element of doubt as to the accuracy of the transcription of this surname. Nevertheless it would seem to record the death of Thomas the son of Thomas and Elizabeth and not the father as they had another son Thomas baptised in 1669]

1667/8 Mar. 24   Elizabeth, daughter to [Tho.] Thomas and Elizabeth Suker, was baptised. [Note that the date is quoted in the old Julian Calendar when March 24 was New Year's Eve, thus Elizabeth was baptised AFTER the death of Thomas.]

1669 Feb. 24   Thomas, son to Thomas and Elizabeth Suker was baptised.
1671 Nov. 14   Thomas Suker, a child, was buried.
1672 Sep. 17   [Abigall] [Abigail], daughter to Thomas and Elizabeth Suker, was baptised

1675 Aug. 1   William, son to Sarah Erdly and Thomas Suker, was baptised.
1676, June 1   Sarah, daughter to Thomas and Elizabeth [Sukar], was baptised.

| 1676 Oct. 23 | Sarah Suker, a child, was buried. [The clerk who originally wrote the register, like many others, was careless in spelling. Here the surname reverts to 'Suker', yet four months earlier it was spelt 'Sukar' for Sarah's baptism.] |

1680 Feb. 3	Josephth Suker, a child, was buried. [The baptism is not recorded so Josephth might have been born only days before.]
1691 Jan. 3	Edward Killume and Elizabeth Shukar, both of this parish, were married.
1704 Dec. 21	Elizabeth, wife of Thomas Suker of Hodnet. was buried.

| 1711 June 23 | Timothy Rodon, of Bowlas, and Abigail Sukar, of Hodnet, both of this parish, were married. [Timothy Rodon also appears in another Mercianotes publication - *The Rodens of Shropshire.*] |
| 1711 Dec. 27 | Thomas Shewker of [Hodnett] was buried. |

| 1800 Apr. 6 | John Suker, of the parish of Drayton, and Amy Ralphs. [presumably of this parish], were married. The wedding was witnessed by Edward Ralphs and Josh. Hughes. |

| 1805 Feb. 14 | William Shuker, of the parish of Stoke, and Ann Powell, [presumably of this parish], were married by licence. The wedding was witnessed by Alice Powell and Thos. Churton. The Minister was Thomas Pigot, |

| 1809 Dec. 28 | William Stokes, of the parish of Drayton, and Sarah Shuker [presumably of this parish], were married. The wedding was witnessed by Mary Stokes and Joseph Hughes. The Minister was Reginald Heber, (Rector) |

Period researched: Baptisms 1540-1812 Marriages 1540-1812 Burials 1540-1812
Reference: Hodnet Parish Register in Lichfield Volume 11 Part 1

Kenley

No members found in this parish.

Period researched: 1682-1812
Reference: Kenley Parish Register in Lichfield Volume 2

Lee Brockhurst

1650 April 28	Richard, son of Ralph and Elizabeth Sukar, was baptised.
1651 March 7	Mary, daughter of Ralph and Elizabeth Sukar, was baptised.
1658 Aug. 22	Ralph, son of Ralph and Elizabeth Sukar, was baptised.

| 1824, Mar. 7 | Thomas, son of John and Elizabeth Shuker of Moston Pool, was baptised by James T. Holloway. John Shuker was a labourer. |

Period researched: Baptisms 1569-1838 Marriages 1569-1838 Burials 1569-1838
Reference: Lee Brockhurst Parish Register in Lichfield Vol 19 Part 4

Longdon upon Tern

No members found in this parish.

Period researched: Baptisms 1692-1812 Marriages 1692-1812 Burials 1692-1812
Reference: Longdon upon Tern Parish Register in Lichfield Volume 2

Montford

No members found in this parish.

Period researched: Baptisms 1573-1812 Marriages 1573-1812 Burials 1573-1812
Reference: Montford Parish Register in Lichfield Volume 7 Part 1

Moreton Corbet

No members found in this parish.

Period researched: Baptisms 1580-1812 Marriages 1580-1812 Burials 1580-1812
Reference: Moreton Corbet Parish Register in Lichfield Volume 1

Moreton Say

1732 Dec. 27	Arthur Suker and Elizabeth Onslow were married.
1800 Feb. 24	Elizth. Shuker was buried.

1796 Mar. 27   John Shaker, of the parish of Newport in the county of Salop, and Jemima Swinchatt, [presumably of this parish] were married by licence. The wedding was witnessed by John Boote and John Swinchatt.

1799 Aug. 11   Jemima Shuker together with Jno. Swinchatt, junr., witnessed the wedding of James Kennerly, and Kitty Swinchatt. The wedding was by licence. The groom was from Trinity Parish, Chester,

1802 May 30   Emma Swinchatt, daughter of John and Jamima Shuker, was baptised.

Period researched: Baptisms 1691-1812 Marriages 1691-1812 Burials 1691-1812
Reference: Moreton Say Parish Register in Lichfield Vol 8 Part 3

Myddle

1824 Mar. 1   Thomas Shuker and Ann Powell were married.

Period researched: Baptisms 1541-1810 Marriages 1541-1810 Burials 1541-1810
Reference: Myddle Parish Register in Lichfield Volume 19

Newtown

No members found in this parish.

Period researched: Baptisms 1779-1813 Burials 1740-1812
Reference: Newtown Parish Register in Lichfield Volume 10

Norton in Hales

1724 June 7   Edward Suker of Drayton and Anna Litler of Drayton {Edvardus Suker de Drayton et Anna Litler de Drayton} were married

1738/9 Jan. 23   Wm. Griffiths and Eliz. Suker were married

Sheinton

No members found in this parish.

Period researched: 1658-1812
Reference: Sheinton Parish Register in Lichfield Volume 2

Stapleton

1691 June 1   Richard Shuker and Priscilla Green were married.
1748 Aug. 5   Wm Rogers and Ann Shuckar were married.
1749 Dec. 26   James, bastard son of Catherine Shuckar, was baptised

1749 Feb. 10   William Shuckar, senr. was buried. [This date is the old Julian calendar when the year changed in March and the burial occurred after the baptism of James.]

1756 Sept 29   William Suker and Richard Oakley witnessed the wedding of Wm Wood, of Cundover, and Elizabeth Oakley. The marriage, which was by licence, was performed by the curate, Thomas Lewis.

1767 Mar. 13   Elizabeth {Eliz[th]} Suker was buried.
1770   [The original register is damaged, but on the 23rd day of a month between April and October in this year a Shuker was buried.]

1779 May 5   Mary Suker was buried.
1796 Aug. 19   Elizabeth Shuker was buried.

Period researched: Baptisms 1635-1812 Marriages 1635-1812 Burials 1635-1812
Reference: Stapleton Parish Register in Lichfield Volume 1

Tibberton

1742 May 23   John, son of John and Catharine Suker, was baptised.
1746 Sep. 15   John Suker, alias Powel, was buried.
1778 Dec. 7   Catherine Suckor, from Besford, was buried.

Period researched: Baptisms 1719-1812 Marriages 1719-1812 Burials 1719 -1812
Reference: Tibberton Parish Register in Lichfield Volume 13

Uppington

No members found in this parish.

Period researched: Baptisms 1650-1812 Marriages 1650-1812 Burials 1650-1812
Reference: Uppington Parish Register in Lichfield Volume 2

Waters Upton

1785 Mar 27   Mary, illegitimate daughter of Elisabeth Shaw, was baptised. Mary's reputed father was Wm. Shuker of Hungry Hatton.
1806 Dec. 30   William, son of Thomas and Mary Shuker of Ellerdine Heath {Elerdine Eath}, was baptised.

1808 May 22   Jane, daughter of Thomas and Mary Shuker of Ellerdine Heath {Elerdine Eath}, was baptised.

1809 Aug. 3.   William, son of William and Ann Shuker of Rowton Lane, was baptised.
1812 June 14   Mary, daughter of William and Ann Shuker of Rowton Lane, was baptised.

1814 Nov. 14   Jane, daughter of William and Ann Shuker of Rowton, was baptised.

Period researched: Baptisms 1547-1812 Marriages 1547-1812 Burials 1547-1812
Reference: Waters Upton Parish Register in Lichfield Volume 13

Wem

1602. Oct. 17   Susanna, daughter of Richarde Suker, was baptised. Richarde was a husbandman.
1605 Feb. 2   Rebecca, daughter of Rycharde Suker, was baptised. Rycharde was a husbandman.

1608 Apr. 23   Anne, daughter of Richard Suker, was baptised. Richard was a husbandman.
1611 Apr. 22   Raphe, son of Richard Suker, was baptised. Richard was a labourer.

1613 June 3	Richard, son of Richard Suker, was baptised. Richard was a labourer.
1616 Jan. 19	William, son of Richard Suker, was baptised. Richard was a husbandman.
1617 June 28	Mary, wife of Richarde Suker, was buried. Richarde was a husbandman.
1618 Aug. 24	Richard Suker and Elizabeth Renolds, (spinster), were married.
1618 Feb. 6	Richard, son of Richard Suker, was buried. Richard was a husbandman. [The date is from the Julian calendar where the year changed in March]
1619 Oct. 6	Rebecca, daughter of William Barnes, was baptised. William was a suker. [This is nothing to do with the Suker family but it was William's occupation and the derivation of the family name being an occupational word for a person who sieved corn by shaking it.]
1619 Jan 2	Mary, daughter of Richard Suker, was baptised. Richard was a husbandman.
1621 Feb. 10	John, son of Richard Suker, was baptised. Richard was a husbandman.
1626 May 14	Richard, son of Richard and Jane Suker, was baptised.
1642 Sep. 24	Richard Suker, a poore man, was buried.
1647 Apr. 25	Jane, daughter of Ralph Suker, was baptised.
1655 Mar. 10	Widow Suker, of Aston was buried.
1681 May 22	Thomas Wells and Mary Suker were married.
1683 Feb. 17	Jane Suker was buried.
1684 July 24	Elizabeth Suker was buried.
1684 Dec. 14	Steven Suker and Elizabeth {Eliz} Rigby were married
1686 Nov. 5	Raph Suker was buried.
1691 Aug. 7	Mary, daughter of Steaven Suker was baptised.
1691 Aug. 21	Mary, daughter of Steaven Suker was buried.
1695 July 30	Jane, daughter of William Sukar was buried.
1696 May 6	William Sukar, of Wem was buried. [The above entry is duplicated three times in different parts of the register with variant spellings of the surname as Shukar and Shuker]
1703 July 2	Elizabeth, wife of Steven Shucker, was buried.
1704 May 25	Stephen Sucker and Shusana Hease, both of this parish, were married.

1711 June 14   Jane Shucker, a widow and a pauper, was buried.
1728 Sep. 14   Stephen Shuker, a pauper, was buried. An affidavit was made.
1739 Jan. 22   Widow Shuker, a pauper, was buried. An affidavit was made.
1744 June 7   Elizabeth Shuker, a spinster, was buried.

Period researched: Baptisms 1583-1812 Marriages 1582-1812 Burials 1582-1812
Reference: Wem Parish Register in Lichfield Vols 9 and 10

Weston under Redcastle

No family members found in this parish.

Period researched: Baptisms 1565-1812 Marriages 1565-1812 Burials 1565-1812
Reference: Weston under Redcastle Parish Register in Lichfield Volume 11 Part 2

Wroxeter

1660 June 5   Abraham Sugar, of ye parish of Upton Magna, and Ales Halle, of this parish, were married.
1661 Apr. 16   Mary, daughter of Abraham and Alice Sugar of Norton, was baptised.
1662 May 11   Alice, wife of Abraham {Suker} of Norton, was buried.

Period researched: Baptisms 1613-1812 Marriages 1613-1812 Burials 1613-1812
Reference: Wroxeter Parish Register in Lichfield Volume 11

Nancy Lindop's Notes

Nancy Lindop has collected some relevant notes on the Shuker family from various sources. These relate to the family in Cheshire.

Alfred Shuker was born at Kynsal Farm 19 April 1897.
His father was Levi Shuker; his mother was Mary Anne Moore.
His Grandfather was John, who was a preacher.
His Great Grandfather was William, who was a groom for the Kilmorys.
Alfred Shuker married Auamalia Lupe in Auckland, New Zealand on 23 May 1925 and had:-
• a son Frederick who married Brenda Bassett;
• a son Alfred, who married Maraea Whareaitu;
• a son Douglas, who married Pauline Stewart;
• a son Robert, who was killed in an accident when he was 5 years old;
• and a daughter Anna, who married Glen Burt, but later divorced.

Alfred's Great Grandfather, William, or Billy as he was known, was at one time a groom for the Kilmory family that owned a lot of land around Audlem. William owned his own house and had a lime works by the side of the canal, which is now part of Kynsal Farm. William kept a few cows on what is still known as Billy's Bank.

Alfred's father Levi, and his mother Mary Anne had six children.
- John Thomas ('Jack') was born on the farm 1890.
- Gertrude was born on the farm 1892.
- Frederick William was born on the farm 1894. He became a butcher.
- Levi, Junior, was born on the farm 1896. He became a farmer.
- Alfred Moore was born on the farm 19 April 1897.
- Amelia was born on the farm 1899.

John Shuker married Ann Simcock at Audlem on 30 June 1814.
Samuel Shuker married Sarah Wilkinson at Audlem on 6 February 1834.

Thomas Suker of Wybunbury married Margaret. They had two daughters; Elizabeth who was baptised on 18 July 1802 and Lucy who was baptised on 15 July 1804.

William Sucker married Hannah Prince at Nantwich on 3 March 1810.

John Sucker married Jemima. Their two sons were baptised at Holy Trinity, Chester, Henry on 14 July 1820 and John on 4 March 1808.

John Sucker married Harriett. Their daughter Harriett was baptised at Holy Trinity, Chester, on 8 February 1810.
The 1861 Census of Cox Bank, Audlem, records John Shuker, an agricultural labourer aged 40, and born in Audlem (1821) was married to 45 year old Emma who was born in Cobridge (1816). They had five children.
- Levi aged 15, born in Audlem (1846).
- Emma aged 9, born in Audlem (1852).
- John aged 7, born in Audlem (1854).
- Thirza aged 4, born in Audlem (1857).
- Ann aged 2, born in Audlem (1859).

John Shuker, a labourer from Checkley married Elizabeth Cadman at Audlem on 1 February 1816. The wedding was witnessed by James and George Cadman. They had the following children.
- Charles baptised 8 June 1817. He became a labourer by 1841.
- John baptised 21 May 1819. He became a cordwainer by 1841. (see below)
- Thomas baptised 9 December 1821.
- George baptised 7 March 1824.
- Mary baptised 21 May 1826.
- Thomas baptised 24 May 1829.
- James baptised 4 December 1831.
- Hannah baptised 23 March 1834.

John Shuker, son of John Shuker (see above) was still a cordwainer in 1861 and by the time of the 1861 Census had married 42-year old Mary Cadman, who was born in Audlem in 1819. They had three children: John William, Elizabeth and Ebenezer.

• John William was born 14 July 1844 in Hunsterson.
• Elizabeth, was described as being born in Wybunbury 1850 on the 1861 Census, but the 1871 Census records her as having been born in the nearby hamlet of Bridgemere. In 1871 she was a dressmaker.
• Ebenezer born 1853 is also recorded as being born in Wybunbury in the 1861 Census and Bridgemere in the 1871 Census.

Bibliography

All the following published by the Shropshire Parish Register Society.

Parish	Publication	Coverage
Adderley	Lichfield Volume 4	Baptisms 1692-1812 Marriages 1692-1812 Burials 1692-1812
Alberbury	Hereford Volume 6	Baptisms 1564-1812 Marriages 1564-1812 Burials 1564-1779
Albrighton nr Shrewsbury	Lichfield Volume 1	Baptisms 1649-1812 Marriages 1649-1812 Burials 1649-1812
Astley	Lichfield Volume 4 part 1	Baptisms 1695-1815 Marriages 1754-1812 Burials 1695-1815
Atcham	Lichfield Vol 14 Part 2	Baptisms 1621-1812 Marriages 1621-1837 Burials 1621-1812
Battlefield	Lichfield Volume 1	Baptisms 1663-1812 Marriages 1663-1812 Burials 1663-1812
Berrington	Lichfield Volume 14 part 4	Baptisms 1560-1812 Marriages 1561-1837 Burials 1560-1812
Cardeston	Hereford Volume 5 Part 5	Baptisms 1678-1706 Marriages 1678-1706 Burials 1678-1706
Clive	Lichfield Volume 8 part 2	Baptisms 1676-1812 Marriages 1676-1812 Burials 1676-1812

Parish	Publication	Coverage
Condover	Lichfield Volume 6 Part 1	Baptisms 1570-1812 Marriages 1570-1812 Burials 1570-1812
Edstaston	Lichfield Volume 10	Baptisms 1713-1812 Marriages 1731-1753 Burials 1712-1812
Fitz	Lichfield Volume 4	Baptisms 1559-1812 Marriages 1559-1812 Burials 1559-1812
Great Ness	Lichfield Volume 20	Baptisms 1589-1864 Marriages 1589-1864 Burials 1589-1864
Grinshill	Lichfield Volume 2	Baptisms 1592-1812 Marriages 1592-1812 Burials 1592-1812
Habberley	Hereford Volume 5 Part 4	Baptisms 1598-1812 Marriages 1600-1822 Burials 1598-1812
High Ercall	Lichfield Volume 20 Part 3	Baptisms 1585-1651 Marriages 1585-1651 Burials 1585-1651
Hodnet	Lichfield Volume 11 Part 1	Baptisms 1540-1812 Marriages 1540-1812 Burials 1540-1812
Kinnerley	St. Asaph Volume 3	Baptisms 1661-1812 Marriages 1661-1812 Burials 1661-1812
Knockin	St. Asaph Volume 3	Baptisms 1673-1812 Marriages 1673-1812 Burials 1673-1812
Lee Brockhurst	Lichfield Vol 19 Part 4	Baptisms 1569-1838 Marriages 1569-1838 Burials 1569-1838

Parish	Publication	Coverage
Llanyblodwel	St. Asaph Volume 3	Baptisms 1599-1812 Marriages 1599-1812 Burials 1599-1812
Llanymynech	St Asaph Volume 8 Part 2	Baptisms 1666-1812 Marriages 1666-1812 Burials 1666-1812
Longdon upon Tern	Lichfield Volume 2	Baptisms 1692-1812 Marriages 1692-1812 Burials 1692-1812
Meole Brace	Hereford Vol 18 Parts 3 & 4	Baptisms 1681-1812 Marriages 1681-1837 Burials 1681-1812
Montford	Lichfield Volume 7 Part 1	Baptisms 1573-1812 Marriages 1573-1812 Burials 1573-1812
Moreton Corbet	Lichfield Volume 1	Baptisms 1580-1812 Marriages 1580-1812 Burials 1580-1812
Moreton Say	Lichfield Vol 8 Part 3	Baptisms 1691-1812 Marriages 1691-1812 Burials 1691-1812
Myddle	Lichfield Volume 19	Baptisms 1541-1810 Marriages 1541-1810 Burials 1541-1810
Newtown	Lichfield Volume 10	Baptisms 1779-1813 Burials 1740-1812
Pontesbury	Hereford Vol 12	Baptisms 1531-1812 Marriages 1531-1812 Burials 1531-1812

Parish	Publication	Coverage
Ruyton of the Eleven Towns	Lichfield Volume 5 Part 2	Baptisms 1719-1812 Marriages 1719-1812 Burials 1719-1812
St Martin	St Asaph Volume 8 parts 2, 3 & 4	Baptisms 1603-1812 Marriages 1603-1837 Burials 1603-1812
Stapleton	Lichfield Volume 1	Baptisms 1635-1812 Marriages 1635-1812 Burials 1635-1812
Tibberton	Lichfield Volume 13	Baptisms 1719-1812 Marriages 1719-1812 Burials 1719 -1812
Uffington	Lichfield Volume 5 Part 1	Baptisms 1578-1812 Marriages 1578-1812 Burials 1578-1812
Uppington	Lichfield Volume 2	Baptisms 1650-1812 Marriages 1650-1812 Burials 1650-1812
Waters Upton	Lichfield Volume 13	Baptisms 1547-1812 Marriages 1547-1812 Burials 1547-1812
Wem	Lichfield Vol 9 &10	Baptisms 1583-1812 Marriages 1582-1812 Burials 1582-1812
Westbury	Hereford Volume 12 Part 2	Baptisms 1538-1812 Marriages 1538-1812 Burials1538-1812
Weston under Redcastle	Lichfield Volume 11 Part 2	Baptisms 1565-1812 Marriages 1565-1812 Burials 1565-1812

Parish	Publication	Coverage
Whittington	St Asaph Vol 2 Part 2	Baptisms 1591-1812 Marriages 1591-1812 Burials 1591-1812
Withington	Lichfield Volume 5 Part 1	Baptisms 1592-1812 Marriages 1592-1812 Burials 1592-1812
Worthen	Hereford Volume 11	Baptisms 1558-1812 Marriages 1558-1812 Burials 1558-1812
Wrockwardine	Lichfield Vol 8 Part 3	Baptisms 1691-1812 Marriages 1691-1812 Burials 1691-1812
Wroxeter	Lichfield Volume 11	Baptisms 1613-1812 Marriages 1613-1812 Burials 1613-1812

Mercianotes specialises in the local history of places in
Cheshire, Shropshire and Staffordshire
and the genealogies of the people who lived there.
Especially the work of Nancy Lindop.
For details of other books in this series
and the rest of the Mercianotes range
please visit the website:

www.mercianotes.com